MW01229005

UNAPOLOGETIC

MANIFESTO

UNAPOLOGETIC
MANIFESTO

To the sex starved, money hungry, disconnected and lonely human race.

OLEG BERSHAD

Restless Mind Publishing

Brooklyn, NY

Copyrighted Material
Unapologetic Manifesto
Copyright © 2017 by Oleg Bershad. All Rights Reserved.

No part of this publication may be reproduced, stored in a retrieval systems
or transmitted, in any form or by any means – electronic, mechanical,
photocopying, recording or otherwise – without prior written permission,
except for the inclusion of brief quotations in a review.

For information about this title or to order other books
and/or electronic media, contact the publisher:

Restless Mind Publishing Inc.
P.O. Box 351165
Brooklyn, N.Y. 11235
www.rmpub.com
www.restlessmindpublishing.com

ISBN: 978-0-9845600-3-5

Printed in United States of America

Written and designed by Oleg Bershad

I dedicate this book to my kids, as my humble attempt

to give them a better world to live in,

than the one that was left for me.

The Essence Of Truth

The Essence Of Truth

(continues)

The oxymoron of loneliness in

the age of communication

RELIGION: Don't Believe The HYPE!

Plan de Vida (Life Plan)

Believing in

impossible as possible...

As we wake up each morning, we face our world of lies and contradictions. Through the course of the day we experience many emotions like fear, love, hate, desire, happiness and misery, hope and disappointment. We feel crowded and lonely all at the same time, but most of all we feel confused. There is no emotion more universal than our confusion with the contradictions that surround us. The world we live in seems like a place that wasn't built for us. There is not one person out there that is completely content with his life. Partially its human nature to be like that, but mainly it's the world that seems out of sorts.

It is impossible to feel safe in this world. We are constantly being scared into submission by wars, diseases and natural disasters. And let's not forget the watchful God, for whom we are a constant disappointment, He scares us the most. Our desires never match with what our world deems acceptable. We are all disgruntling tenants in the apartment building that seems to only work to make us miserable. Each day we drown in a cesspool of our problems and no one is able to help. No one can see the solution, probably because it is right under our noses.

Finally the world seems so cruel and lonely that the only solution we found is denial. Forgetting and ignoring our problems supposed to make us feel happy, but it doesn't. We have not tried honesty yet. We have not tried taking an honest look at our existence.

There is no concept known to us as scary and as liberating as truth. Truth is always there under the surface and whether it is hidden or ignored it is undeniable. We are afraid of truth because our most sacred fears strive on denial. We ask ourselves, am I fat? Am I boring? Am I bad person? We stand in front of the magic mirror: " Mirror, mirror on the wall, am I ...?" And we hope that the mirror never answers!

This oxymoron situation exists, because on one hand we want to know the truth and on the other hand we have to do something about it. If you realize that you are fat and it has been causing you great misery than you have to act. You have to exercise, you have to watch what you eat, and you have to admit that certain failures in relationships came from your enormous size.

What if you truthfully admit that you are a bad person, who was running a corporation with only profit in mind? What if your product is addictive and harmed your consumers, while making you lots of money? What do you do? Do you change your act and give up on huge profits in favor of smaller profits and better products? Do you give back all the money? Truth begs action. It screams at you to be better and work at it. While ignoring truth is a "sweet ignorance" that allows people to commit horrible crimes for their own selfish interests.

One big truth that is constantly ignored, with a purpose, is that all people are equal. The color of your skin or the level of your education doesn't make a lesser human being. Yet for centuries people conveniently ignored this truth as justification of slavery. Almost all religions and nationalistic dogmas preach that different means a lesser person, sometimes even devoid of soul or heart. All this pain is to make few feel like kings and mortal "gods", and most of the time less deserving than the people who serve them. Even today, this warped philosophy is used to oppress and belittle gay people, women, and demographic minorities in any country. Almost every "civilized" country has a group of people that they feel comfortable giving shitty work for low pay and at the same time reserve the right to ridicule them for their differences.

There are many hypocrisies and lies out there and they are very simple to see, when looking at them through the glasses of truth.

Unfortunately for us, we are expert liars. We are always ready to lie for our survival, and as our world grew more complex the lies became bigger and better. Burdened with so many lies, we had to find a solution to keep our sanity. Oddly enough the solution was lying some more, but this time we lied to ourselves. Now we are living in the world where we can't make sense even to ourselves. Like many great liars we forgot the truth about many things and convinced ourselves about our own lies. Now after thousands of years the number of lies is endless and so is the number of problems we face. The lies hurt us badly. They confuse our goals, shutter our dreams and place us in the world that doesn't exist. We live in a real world with real problems, yet we seek solutions in the world created by our lies. It is a terrible disconnect that will bring about our own ruin. If we seek happiness and a better way of living we must recognize the damage created by lies. We must get away from the notion that truth is scary. It is certainly less scary than living in the world that doesn't make any sense. We must learn to embrace the sobering joy of truth. We must use the truth to build a better reality, in which we can live without being afraid of telling the truth. Humanity is in desperate need of truth injection.

AND HERE IS THE FIRST TRUTH: THE WORLD AROUND US IS OUR OWN FAULT.

There is no need to pass the blame on God and act like all we can do is accept our fate. We should stop saying to ourselves that evil always prevails and there is no need to fight a losing war. We should drop the famous excuse that one man cannot change the world. Acting powerless and hopeless is not an acceptable way of living anymore. We, as humanity, are at the crossroads. Our next steps will either make us great or it will make us extinct. The first hard truth is that our messed up world is our own fault. We built the walls, the floor and the roof. We built our own misery, but this is great, because we can fix it on our own too. We have the brainpower and desire to build a better world. The only thing we lack is understanding of what needs to be done.

So how do we begin fixing the world that stayed broken for thousands of years?

We can start by examining ourselves. We can start by asking a very important question: What do we need for a happy existence? We are very complex beings with many levels of needs and wants. We are a complex mix of intellectuality, animal nature, love, hate, intense fear and extreme bravery. The only moment of vanity that is healthy for us to accept is our complexity and not our superiority. We gained our current dominance in this world through our complexity and survival instincts. What makes

4

us special is our ability to find and intellectual solutions to our problems.

So what do we need? What do we want?

The key lies in what I call a "Deserted Island Effect". When a person lands on a deserted island it is a clean slate on life. It is survival at its purest and requires you to be completely honest in your actions. Acting according to your true nature is how you sustain life, and lying or ignoring it can only mean death.

Imagine that you are first people on Earth after the Big Bang. After thousands of years of evolution and many different species of animals and plants, here you stand first group of people. You have thick forests filled with animals and useful plants on one side. You have ocean water filled with fish and sandy beaches on the other side. You cannot walk away from this. It is not a bad dream. It is the reality. It is scary and unforgiving. You have no claws or fangs. You are not even big enough to instill fear. All you have is your nimble brain and hunger for living. If you plan to survive you have to make this situation work for you. You must find a way not to go extinct. This is zero hour for the human race. You can build everything from scratch. And every step that you will take will either propel your race to evolutionary greatness or bring you closer to extinction. When life is brought to its most basic level is how we really show our true nature.

Lets not forget as we take steps to survive we must observe the order in which we take those steps. These steps are the key to the human race and our development. Just like the plants seeking water and sun or animals seeking lush forests or greener pastures, we as a species seek out means of survival and improvement over survival.

I came up with the *PYRAMID* explaining the

EVOLUTION OF HUMAN NEEDS:

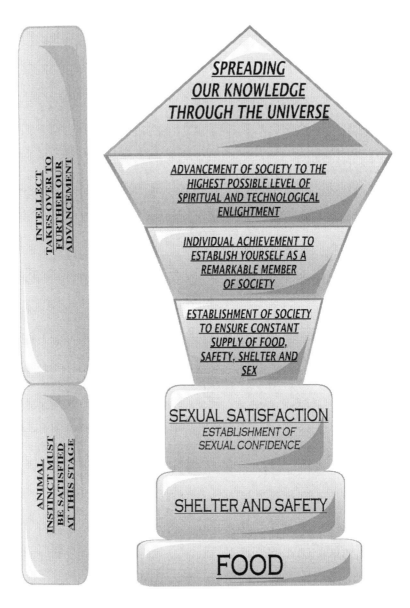

Now that you have taken a look at the pyramid lets explain it step by step. Transform yourself and a group of your male and female companions on to the shore of a deserted island. There you stand naked, hungry, scared and lost. You don't know where you are and what is waiting for you on this island. Lucky for you, it is an early morning and you still have sun that starts to warm up your naked flash. Also to add to your luck, the climate is tropical and you don't have to battle the adversity of foodless, freezing winter.

Your first thought is that you must forage for **FOOD**.

One group will travel into the forest and start looking for berries and edible plants. Scary process like that will even leave some of them dead after consuming poison berries, but they will have to die to save the rest. The second group will gather sharp rocks and collect pieces of wood. They will use some of the smaller rocks to knock down coconuts from a near by coconut tree. If they are really resourceful, they will use wines from near by trees as ropes to attach sharp stones to a straight sticks making spears. They will use these spears to fish and to even hunt. This process will take a whole day. We will suppose that your group is successful on the first day and you have some food to keep you from starving. You even so resourceful that you built a fire and fried up a couple of fishes you caught that day. Fish with coconuts and berries makes your evening feast. You let the fire blow out that night as you fall asleep in the warm sand.

As you wake up the next day you find three of your companions dead and partially eaten by the predators that came from the forest in the night. You bury what is left of your friends underneath a tree. As you travel back to the shore the sky opens into a fierce tropical rain, washing away all the food you collected the day before. As all of your fish and berries disappear into the ocean you realize that food alone was not enough and you must expand your work to ensure **SHELTER AND SAFETY**.

You break your remaining bunch into three groups. One group goes to collect berries and make something to cover up the

7

waistline and vulnerable genitalia. Some palm tree leaves will be fashioned as loincloth. Second group will find more sharp rocks and will try to sharpen them even more. They will make better and more numerous spears. And finally the third group will set out to look for better higher and more protectable shelter. Again we will assume that aside for few setbacks, you are a successful bunch. The third group finds a large cave on a higher ground. Towards the evening all the groups are joined in the cave. They deposit gathered food and build a huge fire at the entrance to the cave. Everyone decides that the fire will be kept going the whole night to keep the predators away. Some will sleep in shifts to keep the fire going.

Next morning you wake up with no food or people missing. So you continue for few weeks learning your island, collecting food and wood. You fashion knives from really sharp rocks and keep the fire alive.

After few weeks or even sooner, the food is steady and you are feeling relatively safe in your cave. You feel like you need to satisfy another urge that was always there and it is called pleasure. Well fed and safe, you start to have sex orgies in the cave. It is everything to you. It is pleasure of the flash, emotional release, entertainment and propagation of your species.

SEXUAL SATISFACTION gives you so much. It makes you connect to each other on a different level. It makes you feel desirable and purposeful. You go from "When will I get off this island?" to "I will make this island my home!" You say to yourself, "My children will remember my great struggle and achieve greatness on this island". More importantly once you reach this stage, you will fight to the death not to go back to being hungry and scared. This stage is your golden prize for surviving the savage surroundings. Now you start working to constantly improve stages one and two, just to make sure that your sexual needs are satisfied. There is no shame in proclaiming your enjoyment of sex. Sex is amazing for a reason, to make our species propagate. If sex was painful and devoid of pleasure, our species will cease to exist in one generation. **SEX AND FOOD ARE TWO NATURAL JOYS WE ARE GIVEN IN THIS WORLD.** And we must have both. Without sex it is feasible that our species will eat themselves to death.

Now let the clock run couple of decades and we have a group of people that now is twice as large as before. You now are unable to fit inside the cave. Your group is so large that some members must sleep outside, also you now have a much higher demand for food. Now you must build a fence to keep people sleeping outside safe and you have to start growing your own food to ensure a constant supply of it. Now you need to ensure the constant supply of food, shelter, safety and sex. You can't rely on chance anymore. Now you have to build, grow and protect on a much larger scale and you can't do it without plan and structure. You must ensure everyone's fare contribution into group and fare sharing of the spoils of labor. Your growing in numbers is a sign of your survival success as a species.

You are in desperate need of *ESTABLISHING A SOCIETAL STRUCTURE*. You will have to set up rules and chores that must be performed to keep your growing need. Builders have to build, hunters have to hunt and cooks must cook food. No one should make others do his or her work, but how can you insure this situation. You put your brightest member in charge. He will oversee all the activities and make sure everyone falls in line. This job will be difficult and privileged and thus you have created your first elected ruler. He will in turn put other bright individuals in charge of smaller tasks to help him. He will recognize how valuable they are and their position will carry the weight of difficulty and privilege as well.

The ruler will always need these individuals to ensure his success, thus he will always promote and single out **INDIVIDUAL ACHIEVEMENT**. A lot of people will try to work harder and shine brighter, to be the members, which are remembered or rewarded or respected more than the others. And on a very healthy level this competition will only make your society better. We will again assume great fortune for your society. We will assume that greed and corruption will never overtake it. We will assume that your society will never split into small warring groups. We will assume that no individual will try to steer people the wrong way for his or hers personal greed. Your society will go on getting bigger and better. It seems like an impossible utopia, but for the sake of argument we will stick to a unified goal.

All men and women united in working for a better future can only lead to one result – better future. Untainted and unified you will develop century after century to become a very advance race. You will achieve amazing technological advances. You will learn your body and your mind to become **ADVANCED SOCIETY** of the future. You will recognize your achievements and you will know that only frontier that left is the endless universe.

You will pack your space ships and send them off into a great nothing to **SPREAD YOUR KNOWLEDGE THROUGH THE UNIVERSE**.

Breathtaking isn't it? We start as cave people and progress into masters of the universe. It is a beautiful dream not a utopia. The difference is that dream can be achieved, all it takes is work and enough people believing in a dream. This dream is not selfish or money driven. In fact it is a goal, which we as a society must strive for. We must be so exemplary that other beings in the universe would want to learn from us.

This pyramid is a helpful guide to a path we can take, but it is also more than that. Each level of the pyramid has to be treated like a building block, a structure which is only strong as its building blocks. Ignore or cheat any of the bottom blocks and the upper blocks will never happen. It is a logical progression in which we first must satisfy our animal nature to give our intellect a chance in advancing our society. Did you ever hear an expression that only people with full stomachs (or rich) can afford morals. On some level we all understand that our basic needs are so important to us, that we would sacrifice anything to satisfy them. People are great mix of animal and intellectual nature. The reason we are not great society yet is that we cheating on pyramid's steps and ignoring the importance of our animal nature.

There is one group of people out there that understand and takes advantage of our animal nature every day, advertisers. They've been linking sex and food to their products for many years. They have been drawing same parallels to men time after time: ALCOHOL=WOMEN=SEX, GOOD FOOD=LARGE PIECES OF MEAT=REAL MEN, SMOKING=SEXY=WOMEN=SEX. They target women just as viciously: QUICK MEAL=HAPPY FAMILY=GOOD MOTHER, SAVY WOMAN=SEXY=MEN. How many times did you watch a commercial almost to the end and still didn't know what they were selling? You were bombarded with images of good-looking people and that placed you in a receptive mode. How many times restaurants paraded images of their food in front of you? They know that good-looking images of food are very pleasurable to our brain. The advertisers know how important food and sex are to us and they use it well to push their products. They know that we will scrutinize every penny when it comes to some of our needs and yet we blindly pay for things that matter to us most.

Unapologetic Manifesto

We never argue the price of a cup of coffee. As long as the coffee is delicious we will pay $5 a cup, knowing that it probably costs no more than a $1 to make. We pay willingly for expensive birth control pills and tablets for erectile dysfunction. Subliminally we all know sex and food matters the most, but only advertisers acknowledge it and use it. So why they have embraced our animal nature and we didn't?

We have spent centuries trying to separate ourselves from our animal nature. We have been on a crazy mission to separate ourselves from something that is a major part of us. Food and sex are basic joys of existence and we are trying to make them relics of our simple past. We searched for justifications, rules, religion to take away our animal urges. And all we left with is guilt! We are constantly feeling guilty for our most natural feelings and desires. We are constantly being told that we will be great human beings if we don't let animal nature control us. ***We always at war with our animal nature, and thus we are at war with ourselves.***

In reality, we have to embrace our animal nature. We have to understand it as part of us and not try to conquer it. Yes we have an animal nature; just like other species we need food and sex. We must accept this and build on this. We must be complete people, which is an animal species with higher brain function. The same body will enjoy a symphony and a sandwich, and both are very important to us to be complete and mentally stable people.

Oleg Bershad

Can our lives be defined by a single word?

At this point I would like to introduce you to an amazing word: **RESOURCE**. Who could have thought, that a word, which simply means a source of supply and support, could define our very existence. It certainly gets a lot of mileage on a daily bases. Businessmen discuss and tally their resources all the time, knowing that they are the foundation of their wealth. Countries go to great length to seek out natural resources that provide them with great political and economic power. Even aliens (according to the movies we make) travel the universe to steal our amazing resources, being it produce, air, water or simply earth to stand on.

This simple word is what determines our history and in it's modesty it is often invisible to the naked eye. It often stays purely in the shadows, hidden behind "great" deeds and lofty ideals. Almost everything we do can be boiled down to this word. Yet, we ignore it a lot too. One of the most visible resources we have is money. And acquisition of money and protection of money takes up so much of our time, that you can say that we live for this resource 24/7. It is a special resource, because money is a human invention. We invented one resource that is capable of buying all other resources on Earth. And even though, we created it, there is not enough of it to go around for all of us. No wonder people cheat, lie, and kill to get their hands on this amazing invention. Money is such a powerful resource that it blinded most of us into thinking that it is really the only resource we need. It seems that many things in our life fall into place once we acquire large sums money.

Still I would argue that money is meaningless. It is an artificial resource that we all agreed upon and it is only a resource while we have use for it and believe in it. Money wasn't always around, but once we invented it, money quickly became a simple way to exchange resources. We decided to measure all are useful resources in the increments of useless resource called money and the barter system got an amazing upgrade. At the same time, we started a long process of distancing ourselves from real resources and concentrating on the fake ones. Here lies a real danger for humanity. Our understanding of our resources shapes the society we live in and sets us on a certain path. We are living organism, whose survival depends on resources and we cannot ignore them anymore. Many man-made inventions brought human race to the point at which we will have to choose our future quickly and correctly. Understanding and protecting our resources is a very key to our survival.

It is not by accident that the two bottom blocks of the **"EVOLUTION OF HUMAN NEEDS PYRAMID"** consist of food, shelter and safety. Food and water are our most important resource that keeps us alive. They are very important to us, organic beings. What if food and water was not available to all of us? Or what if there is a shortage that could only sustain one quarter of people on Earth? What will happen to us? Will the remaining ¾ of the population have to die? Are we really keeping good tabs on food and water? Do we even have a plan for survival of our species? And finally, are we aware of how close we are to running out food and clean water to support all of us?

It might not be obvious, but we, as people, are also a resource. We are a living organism and a machine in constant production. We produce food, build, invent technological wonders, and produce more people. What is very interesting is that we are a kind of resource that as we get greater in numbers we become a burden upon ourselves. In a way, we are victims of our own success. **AS WE BECOME BETTER AT SURVIVAL AND MORE AND MORE OF US SURVIVE, WE HAVE TO FIND A SOLUTION TO US.**

Despite numerous and brutal wars, diseases and natural disasters Earth population is growing. Our evolutionary resilience, which once made us exceptional, is now putting us in danger. Many experts agree on the fact, that overpopulation is a serious problem. Each of us living, breathing, having kids is putting a strain of the Earth's limited resources. Roughly speaking Earth population went from couple of hundred millions after 1 A.D. to almost 7 Billion in 2016 and growing. During World War II (1940s) we were just over 2 billion. The population rose by 5 billion people in less than a 100 years. While Earth itself cannot increase in size to accommodate all of us, it is still arguable if we reached the critical point or how long it will take until we get there   For example, a British scholar and economist Thomas Robert Malthus, as far back as 1826, published his *An Essay on the Principle of Population*. In it he claimed that Population growth is exponential, while food production growth at arithmetic rate. Thus he predicted that population growth will outrun food production. In turn shortage of food will lead to unemployment, starvation, crime and war. Many experts today claim that reaching the population of 10 to 11 billion people on Earth is beyond the capacity of Earth to feed us all.

Unapologetic Manifesto

According to United Nations' The World Population Prospects: 2015 Revision, the world population will reach 8.5 billion by 2030, 9.7 billion in 2050 and 11.2 billion in 2100. (www.un.org)

An oxymoron to the above statistic is our consumption. We consume resources at a much higher rate, regardless of our large numbers. Our consumption is so large, that some experts claim that consumption is the major cause of the environmental problems we face.

The Journal of Industrial Ecology printed a study in December 2015 called "Environmental Impact Assessment of Household Consumption". The study shows that household consumption contributes to more than 60% of global green house gases (GHG) emissions and between 50% to 80% of total land, material, and water use.

Another example of overconsumption or improper consumption is a serious rise in obesity. It is only natural to expect that with increase of the population the quality of food will drop. Foods high in fat, sugar, and cholesterol will rule the constantly expanding (and mostly strained on cash) market to satisfy the demand. The most recent data I found was from 2014.

According to World Health Organization (www.who.int): In 2014, more than 1.9 billion adults, 18 years and older (39%), were overweight. From these 600 million (13%) were obese.

41 million children under the age of 5 were overweight or obese in 2014.

According to International Diabetes Federation (www.idf.org) 2015 data:

In 2015, 415 million people had diabetes (1 in 11 adults). And they project in 2040, 642 million (1 in 10 adults) will have diabetes.

There will be people out there claiming that these statistics are alarmist or not indicative of a possible doom. Yet consider this, from 1940s to 2050s the population will rise almost five times. It doesn't matter what exact number will cause us to reach capacity or will tip the scale to our self-destruction. Without any real global plan, the doom might come quicker or will be irreversible when it comes. What concerns me the most is not getting there, but how will we get there. **WHAT WILL BE OUR SOLUTION TO US?** Will it be cruel and merciless or will it be a thought out plan that will try to save us all? Even now we live in the world, which allows itself to turn away from suffering of others, we let the distance act as our moral compass. If people are starving, living without clean water, or are dying of a horrible disease we let it be, if it is far away. Or we use the oldest childish trick in the book, if we don't see it than it can't be happening.

It is worth noting, that even now while food and clean water still exist, it only exists for some. According to World Food Programme (www.wfp.org) and The Hunger Project (www.thp.org):

795 million people – or one in nine people in the world – do not have enough to eat to lead a healthy active life.

Poor nutrition causes 45% of death in children under five, which is about 3 million children lost each year.

According to Center for Disease Control and Prevention (www.cdc.org) and (www.unwater.org) 2013 data:

780 million people do not have access to clean water

2.5 billion people do not have access to adequate sanitation

These are staggering statistics for the world that considers itself civilized and advanced. And of course, many people will use a dirty term "developing countries", and say that majority of starvation and problems with clean water is limited to those countries.

My question is why do we allow the existence of developing

countries and don't help them with development? It is because the world still operates according to ancient clan system. Each country exists in its own microcosm and strives to be better than rest. There is very little motivation out there to make life equally decent for the whole world. We still only are concerned with problems that happen under our noses, but what we must realize is that airplanes erased all of that. A disease in one place of the world, which came out of a contaminated water supply, can get on the plain and reach even the furthest parts of the world in 24 hours. New transportation modes made it easier and faster to travel. They also made the world smaller and made it necessary to think globally. Humanity is only as strong as its weakest link. And with overpopulation and our dwindling resources the whole human race is under a threat. We always monitoring scary disease like Ebola and AIDS as a possible cause of our annihilation, but we also must understand that decline in the world resources like food and water are just as scary.

Before we get to global solutions of dwindling resources, we must first fully grasp how resource determine the world we live in. I propose a theory, that all people are born 80% good and they try not to act on the other 20%. Unfortunately, when people live in the environment that is scarce on resources, they become scarce on humanity. The balance starts to become 60/40, 50/50, or even 20/80. ***THERE IS A DIRECT CORRELATION BETWEEN RESOURCES AND HUMANITY, OR THE LEVEL OF BENEVOLENCE, WITH WHICH WE LIVE.*** Fortunately for us there is great example that we can observe in animal kingdom and apply it to our world.

In fact, if we take a look at bonobo and chimpanzee monkeys we can learn a lot about our behavior, by seeing how resources have shaped them to be very different from each other. Their genome is very close to human and thus can provide us with a very great insight. What is amazing about them is that in Africa they live very close to one another, living on opposite sides of Congo River, yet the availability of resources pushed them in developing two very different societal structures. In general human world is often compared to chimpanzee monkeys and bonobos to human hippies. Some scientists believe that their difference lies in small differences in genetic code, thus making it something they are born with. I see it somewhat different. I want to propose a point of view where they are a product of their environment more than their genetics. The available resources and difference in threats to their life caused them to be very different.

First let's start with gentle bonobo monkeys. Their habitat is confined to specific area south of the Congo River in the Democratic Republic of Congo. They exist in the area abundant with food and their main predators are people and crocodiles. And people are really their major threat. Compared to Chimps their existence is very sheltered and less dangerous. As a direct response to abundant resources and limited danger they have developed a very peaceful society. Some claim they lack development and have a juvenile brain. Yet there is no lethal aggression in their society and they mate across the community lines. Their society learned not to kill their own. Can we claim that as people? Obviously, not! They don't see each other as a threat and it is a big plus in my book. To show how not afraid they are, they have great tolerance for strangers and as they settle in their trees they shout to each other before bedtime as a kind of good night ritual. Just think about the good night ritual as one of the most humane experiences in our lives and bonobos have it. As we enter the unknown darkness of sleep, people we love acknowledge their love and presence, and they reassure us that we will see them again with the new light. For bonobos it is a very dangerous practice, since it announces their position to a possible predator. Yet, they practice it anyway. They are more empathetic to each other and more willing to share resources. They also don't have violent conflicts between groups and are generally able to control their emotions.

In fact, they live in a society dominated by females. They raise children communally with no claims to fatherhood. And they use sex as greeting, conflict resolution, and generally a way to reduce the tension. Sex is often non-reproductive and frequently homosexual especially in females. I know that such sexual freedom seems very scary to the majority of humanity, but maybe bonobos found something we didn't. Maybe beings who have abundant food and sex tend to be happy. And happy people or monkeys don't think about killing and value life much more, because their life is good.

So here we have a society living on abundant resources and minimal threat that spends its days gathering food and literally loving each other. It might seem simplistic, utopian and unrealistic to our human ears. Yet they exist in peace and security we can only dream off. The only reason their numbers are declining, is human beings eating them and selling them to the zoos. They themselves are 90% vegan and almost never hunt for meat. Did I say vegan, sex-loving monkeys? No wonder people have been comparing them to hippies.

If you found bonobos life style shocking, you will find comfort in chimps. Their existence, much like ours, forced them to fight for their resources and avoid numerous threats. Starting with North of Congo River chimps are spread to many areas East, West and Central Africa. Their habitat is diverse and the food is not as abundant. Limited food resources forced chimps to be greater hunters and often praying on young antelopes or goats, colobus monkeys and blue monkeys. In addition they face multiple threats like humans, leopards, lions, crocodiles and large pythons. Although their adversity caused them to develop the opposable thumb and made them great with tools, their world is very violent.

Since there is not enough resources to go around, physical force becomes a major decider of the societal structure. Alpha males rule their society and they form groups and alliances. They often violently protect their territory and attack other groups. Does that sound familiar to our world?

In the society where resources are scarce and dangers are many, strength dominates everything. Alpha males control and protect the resources and in return are given a bigger piece of the pie. The chimp sexual behavior is mainly of reproductive nature, they have clear fatherhood and also a lot of instances of infanticide. I by no means suggest that this is a direct relationship between scarce resources and infanticide, but infanticide is not an issue for bonobos.

While in bonobo society females enjoy equality and superiority, which doesn't bother abundantly sexed bonobo males even a bit, the chimp females became a commodity or another resource. Alpha males protect them and monopolize them.

It is extremely important to understand, that in a society scarce on resources being Alpha male is a definition of success. You can even paraphrase it and say that whoever is the biggest asshole, is considered a success. This individual is guaranteed to eat better and have more and better sex. It also means that the ones he is protecting are definitely getting much less, but are still thankful for their leftovers and his protection. What is shocking, that in this societal structure females are no longer considered full members of the society. They are more like a sexual resource to procreate and please Alpha males and, if not so "lucky", please other lesser males in the group. This kind of structure dehumanizes women, making them a thing or a prize. The quality of female companion defines the level of success achieved by an Alpha male, turning her into just one of his prize trophies.

Fear of death in a strained environment, gives power to Alphas and makes a lot of Alpha-centric groups which keep fighting for more power and access to resources. Which makes for a lot misery, fear, unequal distribution and frustration. You cannot live a normal existence always looking over your shoulder or even worse give power to an asshole and wonder why he is not sharing. Even more shocking is the air of constant competition that exists for resources. If members of your society compete with you for necessities, there is no love, no sharing, and no empathy. If your competitor dies, it automatically means more for you. Ironically, even the life of the Alpha male is not great, because he constantly must fight to maintain his superiority. It is a popular belief that competition provides a healthy drive forward, pushing people to be better. I agree, competition is great when you are trying to design a better watch, bake a better cake, or trying to design a better spaceship. Competing for resources like food and clean water we create a world with lots of angry, marginalized, dehumanized, and forgotten people. In short, it is a world of less than 10% "winners" and a whole lot of "losers". Do we really want to live in the world where misery rules our daily lives?

Personally I prefer living as a bonobo than a chimp.

It is hard to ignore the importance of food, water and shelter as our main resource for survival. As basic as they seem, it feels almost an impossible task to fix those two pillars of pyramid at this point in our history. Don't get me wrong I am very optimistic about the future, but I also must recognize that progress and change are hard for people. Too many Alpha males have turned themselves into happy kings and they will not be easy to turn. The world in which everyone is mostly happy is a new and strange concept to put through. For thousands of years it was, few happy at the expense of the others as a way to survive. And when misery becomes a norm, it is a difficult work to free a slave happy with his chains. It is even more difficult to ask a king to give up his throne in the name of universal happiness.

I did come up with some important solutions that we might need to implement fast. It feels like we might be running out of time to fix our world. I will discuss these solutions later in the book. Simply because any good solution requires drastic changes in the way we live. First I want to concentrate on pillar number 3, Sexual Satisfaction. I feel like maybe fixing our sexual lives will create a miracle of happy individuals that might want to make the world around them a better place. Plus it feels like the only pillar that can be fixed without a major war.

We as humanity have no natural predator at this time. Animals are no longer a threat to us. And since a lot of our communities have food and water, our bad sex lives are our own fault.

The self-inflicted rules and repression has made our sexual behavior very strained. Our mating rituals and the way we look for mates has become very complex, with a very low probability of success. And if eating and fucking are really two main joys for an organic organism, what happens when you take away the fucking? At the very least you have an obesity epidemic, and at the most you have anger and frustration. Anger and frustration becomes violence, which leads to killing and more misery.

Sexual Satisfaction is so important to our existence that it deserves libraries of books and billions in research to make it better and even more enjoyable. In my conversations with many adults, I find tremendous gaps in knowledge of sex and love.

These adults often have no idea of basics and thus pay dearly for each mistake in judgment or gap in knowledge. And let's be honest, gaps in knowledge are the leading cause of bad judgment. I myself constantly discover new aspects of this wonderful process and try to find ways to be better.

Finding a needle

in a haystack

Sexual Satisfaction, as described by the Evolution Of Human Needs Pyramid, is establishing of your sexual confidence through normal and abundant sexual practices. Unfortunately our sexual satisfaction is not guaranteed at all, but sexual frustration is a given. There are so many misconceptions, over and under examinations of our sex life. There are so many nuances and different schools on what our sex life should be. I will not attempt to cover them all, rather try to remove the chains that bind us to our frustration.

Lets assume that we are "free" to choose our mate. From the very start the process already has enormous embedded difficulties to it. I want to introduce another diagram I call Circles Of Prejudice. In it I try to show different things that are preventing you from meeting someone you desire and will be happy with. From billions people on Earth you have to find one person, who will satisfy ALL your sexual and emotional needs; one person with whom you will tie your life for its entire duration. If this person exists, it cannot be an easy process to find this needle in a haystack.

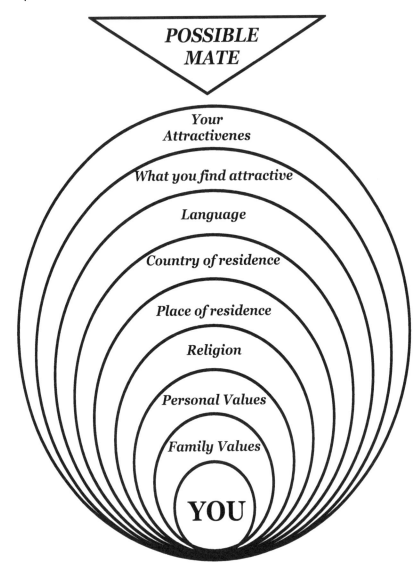

CIRCLES OF PREJUDICE

There on a distant horizon is your perfect soul mate. He or she is visible yet not reachable, separated by many invisible walls that society has created. Out of all the people in this world we are forced to choose between a limited few and hope that this limited group holds a person that will make us happy. First, this magical person has to live somewhere near you. Then you have to speak the same language so you can communicate to each other your thoughts and desires. Then this person must believe in your God. He or She should be brought up with same prejudice your parents forced on you. Then this person must act according to the social norms. And then this person must be sexually attractive to you. Finally when all this is satisfied, you must satisfy the requirements that this other person has. Talk about an almost impossible task to achieve. On top of this we are constantly being told that there is going to be just one and only person who will ring your bell. No cheap substitutes will do. This person was born so you can make each other happy and all you have to do is find this magical person. You have to find this one and only person among 7 billion strangers. Good luck. It is an enormous amount of pressure and anxiety that we ourselves put on the process, that should be much simpler and more enjoyable. Yet currently it is anything but. There are industries that make millions of dollars on our matting process. Some work on trying to bring us together like dating websites, speed dating, and never dying art of match making. Some profit on our joys and eventual misery, like marriage or divorce. We even have marriage and relationship counseling, because we feel that a third party will understand something that we cannot understand ourselves. We have numerous books, poems, and movies trying to understand or mating habits. Still we are not any closer to a solution. Finding a right person to be with should be enjoyable, not terrifying.

Believe it or not our misery begins from childhood, with

those seemingly harmless tales we have been told so many times as kids. Yes, I am talking about Fairy Tales, or I like to call them "The Amazing Adventures of an Alpha Male". One of my favorite jokes goes like this: "Women spend years waiting for a prince on a white horse. And when he finally arrives, they usually prefer the horse!"

Think is through, prince is a rich Alpha male that is able to slay any dragon and must marry a princess. And this princess must be the fairest in the land and also incredibly passive. She is not even trying to escape the dragon or a wicked sorcerer who is guarding her. She is just sitting in her tower, brushing her hair and waiting for prince to arrive.

So for a man, your role model is a prince. He must be rich, how else he can afford a dress for his princess, a white horse and a greatly expensive wedding at the end. He must be athletic and strong to slay the dragon. He shouldn't have a real job which could keep him from riding his horse for month looking for a princess and then spend endless time writing and reading poems to her. He also must have a woman, more beautiful than any other woman around. He is an Alpha and the beautiful woman is his prize. Isn't this a description of an average asshole kid from a rich family, who never did any serious work in his life? A selfish a quest with a selfish prize, during which numerous animals and witches and dragons die. If this is not a scary ideal to put inside the child's head, what is even scarier is that only a small percent of men becomes Alpha males. The rest of us must feel like losers or even worse villains in the fairy tale. In reality, prince and princess fairy tales is an old time (pre-books and pre-TV) version of "Lifestyles of rich and shameless".

For women it is even worse. Which is totally understandable and despicable, when you talking about the "Amazing Adventures of an Alpha Male". These fairy tales paint resourceful women as wicked and dangerous, while obedient and almost catatonic is praised as a virtue. A prince has to battle adversity to get his princess based on his many "exceptional" qualities. The princess on the other hand just has to be the fairest in the land, that's all. Sure she must love all forest creatures, and she does, conveniently excluding all the ones that can eat her. Her personality is never in question. She is expected to be nice, which I assume is easier when you never had any real hardship or had never worked a day in your life.

Even those things are minor compared to what fairy tales do about woman's perception of her own beauty. One thing we all know is that you cannot fight your genes. As much as modern science has done for us, our faces is something we have to deal with our entire life. Yet, most of European fairy tales praise being blond, or "angel" like, as more beautiful than being brunette. And being a red head is considered almost strange and unnatural. Facial moles or facial hair are treated as straight up signs of being a witch. Also facial features that are less gentle or belonging to a minority group are considered enough to label you as a witch. In fact, hooked nose, dark hair and dark eyes were enough as your witch credentials. In actuality, many fairy tales made a dangerous parallel. They made DIFFERENT=UGLY=WITCH=EVIL=NOT WORTHY OF LIVING. Princesses never have any meat on their bones. They are always skinny and frail, practically malnourished and dying. There are certainly no plus size princesses.

Of course, not all the fairy tales are bad. A good number of them teach us valuable lessons, like not to sit on the wall or we might break. They teach us to know our relatives by face, so we can tell the difference between them and a forest wolf. They teach us that a house of stick and straw will never withstand a hurricane and brick is the way to go. Even for all the good old time racism, fear of minorities, and insane preoccupation with acquisition of wealth, some fairy tales bare important life lessons. Some good ones teach you not to be greedy, some teach the importance of following your heart and some simply teach kids not to follow a stranger offering candy into his van (or secluded mid-forest spooky looking house).

Still I propose, that prince and princess fairy tales do the most damage done to our psyche. They are first ways we are introduced to relationships and the way we perceive happiness. They set very specific standards on being male or female, as we discussed above. And they set marriage as the ultimate goal and prize of any relationship. It unconsciously sets goals and standards that the real world offers to very few and leaves the rest in a bitter disappointment. Of course fairy tales are not alone in that, which takes us to those pesky and dangerous words we use daily.

First comes Romance, Sex, Love,

and Marriage...

And before you know it,

you're pushing a baby carriage!

Words are just words. Take any word and repeat it 30 times, and it will become just a sound. This sound will loose its meaning with every pronunciation. It is very simple. Words are meaningless. We are the ones who give them meaning. We are the ones who make them important. We are the ones who decide that these words should define our daily existence. And we are the ones responsible for the misery caused by some of these words. I would like to discuss four of these words, which we didn't define well. Yet these four words define all interactions between men and women:

Romance, Sex, Love, and Marriage.

These four words put tremendous value on trivial and deemphasize or even demonize all the meaningful aspects of our lives. It is very curious thing; we all have our natural instincts and desires we always dwarf as evil. It seems we have a down right war on human nature. Everything that feels natural is considered an animal-like and a primitive instinct, that for some reason we have to repress. We somehow think that the more distant we are from our animal nature, the closer we are to being civilized and mental enlightenment. It is extremely wrong and dangerous to think of this as black and white, when our reality works best when it is gray. When it comes to our relationships, nature already provided us with many tools and instincts to propagate our species. All we have to do is understand and embrace who we are.

Yet the artificial words we have created, and often contradictory to our nature, have become our "natural" understanding of our relationships.

There is nothing wrong to being sweet to each other. There is nothing wrong with feeling empathy towards other people and caring for one another. Pleasant and unpleasant feeling arise all the time and they are natural. As people we naturally lean towards good feelings and enjoy them more. We strive to like more and more the world around us. I know it is harder to come by each day, but remember we are living in the environment that sets us up for misery, hate and failure. Fixing the way we interact with one another can set us up for more joy and understanding.

Like I said before, it is natural to care about another human being or a group of human beings. It is natural to sexually desire another human being or beings. It is even more natural to care about and desire a single person intensely, and this is the strongest emotion we feel as people. When both of these connect in one individual, our world becomes totally focused on them. We naturally want to please this individual that connected these two emotions in us. We want to please this person sexually. We want to surround him or her with maximum care and attention. We genuinely care about this person's likes or dislikes, favorite music and food. We want to take this person to places that make this person feel happy. Simply if they are happy with us, we are happy too. Moreover, we want this magical person to feel like they found magic in us, which we all know is hard to come by. Feeling that you found in each other both feelings of care and desire is great and often people just try to get by on one feeling alone. Some people, mainly nurturing females, try to get by on care alone. I care about him and that is enough to stay with him. Sometimes people try to get by on just intense desire. Desire seems to bind people stronger than care. The reason is when searching for a mate desire is our primary guide. After all, we care about our family and friends, yet we don't want to have sex with them.

And finally sometimes, we find both feelings in one person and then loose one of them or both. Unfortunately this does happen often, where we care but don't desire anymore or desire and find it impossible to continue caring. This might seem horrible, but remember our world is fluid and ever changing. **IT IS CRAZY TO THINK THAT AS THE WORLD CHANGES, WE WILL REMAIN THE SAME.** We evolve and change all the time. And just like our food tastes change, so does our taste in people. We all have somebody in our lives, who seemed perfect once, flawless even. Yet, now they seem totally different and might be even repulsive. What happened? One of you changed or even both changed as people. And this is a normal process; it is abnormal to try to ignore its existence.

Care and desire lived for millions of years and it exists in humans as well as animals. It never required a definition or specific word that would describe it. These are the two basic emotions that guided us for a long time, and just few centuries ago we felt a need to put a label on these emotions. We created words that describe ideal relationships and decided that they are norm for our existence. Think about it, we made up words and called them important and decided that these words will rule our relationships and daily lives. **WE GAVE THESE WORDS VAGUE DEFINITIONS AND THUS CREATED CONFUSED MASSES, WHICH STRIVE FOR SOMETHING NOBODY CANNOT DEFINE FOR SURE.**

Unapologetic Manifesto

We are searching for the greatest treasure of all, yet we don't know what it looks like exactly. Thus, we don't know if we found it or lost it or never encountered it. No wonder we think that our world sucks.

The first word I want to take a look at is the word *ROMANCE*.

Romance by definition (as it refers to love) describes a feeling of excitement and mystery associated with love or everyday life, which is remote from everyday life. Also the words used to describe it are exaggerated, invented story, sentiment, something extravagant without a basis in fact. To the great credit of the dictionaries they honestly provide the definition, which is a true origin of the word, even though most of us don't know it at all.

The word Romance is derived from 1300s French word "romanz", meaning "in the speech of the people", "the vulgar tongue" or written "in the Roman style" as opposed to Latin. The word derived from Latin word Romanice. It was supposed to be stories made more accessible to everyone, being that it wasn't written in Latin. It must be noted, that as a genre it was developed in aristocratic courts in the dawn of Renaissance. There was a general feeling among the intellectuals of that time, that humanity hasn't progressed much since Greeks or Romans. Thus this stagnant period needed a revival, which literature was meant to inspire. The **ROMANCE LITERARY GENRE** originally came to imitate Greek stories of chivalry and was meant to create fiction about chivalry and love of medieval knights. These stories were meant to be idealized, extravagant, and **HAVE NO CONNECTION TO REALITY.**

So lets be clear about. Romance started in rich, intellectual circles as fictional stories made for entertainment and amusement. It was not meant to instill morality or be anything more than entertainment written in accessible language and filled with events and people detached from reality. Initially it was all about knight and heroic battles and quests, and no romantic love or love affairs what so ever. Also since the creation of printing press in 1440 the Romance genre received a boost needed to spread these stories around the world.

In the modern day and age Romance is a big business, which includes romantic novels, romantic poetry, and romantic movies. Of course all of them claim to be the modes of entertainment, but they became much more. Just like the fairy tales we discussed earlier on the surface they seem harmless. The problem is that now men and women draw their standards from these works of entertainment. Unfortunately, we love stories, but all good stories have a fatal flaw. **IN ORDER FOR A STORY TO BE FUN IT MUST HAVE A DYSFUNCTION IN IT.** All stories, which have normal interaction, are boring, because they are normal.

For example, he met her they treated each other with respect, they pleased each other sexually on a regular bases, they never lied to each other and never cheated on one another. Together they acquired considerable wealth, five adorable kids, who love and admire their parents all the time. And they lived in the period of peace and prosperity, never knowing horrors of war or hunger. Boring right? Normal is often boring, so stories pack themselves with dysfunctional and mentally damaged people to make it fun. After watching few episodes of soap operas, you start to realize that all these characters need is to be in one room together. If you had them all together and they all spilled their guts it would be over in one episode and 80% of them will go on having happy lives.

Even recently a slew of very popular TV shows have created a culture of young people that easy to observe living in New York City. These shows made Manhattan into a playground for kids of rich parents. Also they have poor young professional cramming themselves in tiny overpriced apartments for a chance to live as swinging single in Manhattan. Young women flock by thousands to receive their martinis and gay male friends at the entrance to the island. And young men flock by thousands to meet these metropolis girls, who baldly admit their desire for love and romance, while going through hundreds of blind dates and one night stands. After all, their favorite characters also didn't get married or stayed with someone for too long. Something always made it impossible, like unrealistic expectations, their inability to cope with another person in their apartment or just shortage of princes and white horses.

Just like anyone out there, I am a big fan of some of the movies and some of the TV shows. What makes me different is an ability to draw a line between reality and "TV and book reality". It seems that many people cannot draw that line and understand that blending unrealistic fiction with real life is a disaster.

Lets start with one important part of Romance as it pertains to us. Since it started in medieval times and had its bases in Greek literature, there is this notion of the "good old days". The notion of great romance and heroic deeds, to which man of today unable to aspire. Of course, man can claim the shortage of dragons and a cell phone replacing a sword on their belt. The main problem is that good old days weren't that good. In fact they were pretty disgusting and horrible both to men and women.

Just for fun, as we dive into our past for a tiny bit, remember that Shakespeare lived from 1564 to 1616. This is the time that he wrote "Romeo in Juliet" at the height of Renaissance. The man, who wrote one of the greatest romantic plays, didn't use toilet paper. One of the basic hygiene products we take for granted, was not around for public use in Shakespeare's lifetime.

Historically Greeks used stones and clay. Romans used a sponge on a stick in a bucket of highly salted water and the bucket was for *communal* (this is even nasty to imagine, let alone try) use. As the matter of fact, the first toilet paper was commissioned by Chinese emperor in Song Dynasty around 1300s, but was never available to the public. First flush toilet was invented Sir John Harrington in 1596, but didn't appear commercially until 1800s. Even colonial Americans used leaves, newspapers, and pages of Farmer's Almanac. In US, the first toilet paper appeared in 1857 as Gayetty's Medicated Paper. Yes, those sweet smelling "good old days", just don't get any better than a communal sponge on a stick.

If previous two paragraphs didn't put a damper on romantic "good old days", lets talk of toothbrushes and toothpaste. Some form of toothpaste was always around, but people used some weird stuff in it. Historically we used anything we found to be abrasive we thought would work. We used ashes, burned eggshells, crushed bones, oyster shells, charcoal and bark. Until as recent as 1945, toothpaste had soap in it and it was powder for the most of twenties century. Toothbrush first modern design appeared in 1780. Before that chew sticks with frayed end and from aromatic trees is what people used. There was some kind of toothbrush from 1400s using animal hair as bristles, but it was a luxury not available to everyone. Only after the invention of nylon by Dupont Labs in 1938, we started to use toothbrushes as they are today.

So, the toilet paper and toothpaste and toothbrushes as we know them today are very recent inventions. It is interesting to think that all those heroic knights and sexy ladies of "good all days" where running around with smelly asses and bad breath. I dare you to read any romantic novel involving knights or king's court and think about anything else, but the fun they had with their hygiene.

If hygiene issues were not enough, "good old days" had other monumental problems. First, during the Renaissance period life expectancy for both men and women was in their mid-forties. That's right, all of you people who are beginning your life at forty according to the "good old days" would be dead. Second, women usually married in their teens and had on average 5 to 7 or even 10 kids. If that wasn't enough, childbirth was so dangerous that women often died giving birth. Dying during childbirth was so common that women usually wrote out their wills once they got pregnant. And the horrors don't end here, almost 20% of all children died before the age of five from various reasons like diseases, starvation, infanticide, poverty and good old-fashioned brutal wars.

Yes constant wars, rapes, pillaging and mysterious diseases plagued the human kind are much worse than anything we face today. Of course, we tend to forget these facts and romanticize the past endlessly. As far as I am concerned, I am very happy with a more civilized now.

I want to make couple more point about romance stories. Majority of them is set in a rich community and by all means could be called "Sex adventures of rich and shameless". We are still fascinated by this rubbish somehow till this day, which explains the obsession with reality TV and celebrity lives. I don't know if our own lives are so boring, but I never thought to care about whom celebrities fuck or marry. Remember in those "good old days" the class lines were drawn with a very fat marker. What was happening to the peasants or servants who were mere satellites around the rich? Were their stories "romantic"? I doubt it, especially when it involved rich lords and ladies. They had constant, meaningless sex with servants and peasants. As the matter of fact, many poor women were raped at will, with no punishment or consequences of any kind to the men who did it. There was an abundance of bastard children, who had to grow up rich-adjacent and die in poverty like their mothers. It probably, would not be uncommon for a rich lord to have sex with his servant girl and then sit down and write a sonnet "to his lady love". And have the same servant girl, maybe even pregnant; carry this sonnet to the "rich lady love", inviting the last one to meet under the stars in the garden.

There are many great sex scenarios we could think of that get us hot in that context. Rich woman and a stable boy, probably implying that he is hung like a horse. Lord and his shy servant girl, who cannot believe her luck of being ravaged while she is changing her lords dirty sheets. Greek orgies that involved numerous sexual explorations and gave ideas to the porn industry of today, all seems tantalizing until you remove the shroud of bullshit from them. In reality, rich lords and ladies utilized poor people heavily for their sex needs and discarded them as low class people. Meanwhile, they wrote love poems and spend hour wooing other lords and ladies. The hypocrisy of these romances is staggering and it is a lie that doesn't nearly describe the lives of 90% of us living in this world.

There are so many silly concepts that came out of romantic stories. One of them is "To die for love". Sounds romantic as hell, except who will be left to love. A corpse is a terrible companion. And does a person really have to die to prove his or her love? Wouldn't the person's presence to care and sex up the other person be better, then a stupid gesture? Shouldn't we aspire to live for love? Of course this dying business, came out of another silly concept like "Longing and being separated from love". There are many romantic stories based on a constant angst of wanting to be with somebody and yet they cannot be near, because they are fighting a war or on a quest. The man get to fight windmills and women get to sigh longingly, while staring out the window and clutching a handkerchief he gave her before he left. When you really, honestly think about it, all these feelings are really about the unrealized sexual desire. And sex, I've been told, requires physical presence. Again while they are longing and dying, these lords and ladies survive by screwing their help and visiting abundant whorehouses. Meanwhile they remain "pure" for each other. Here is fun thought, a quest in our time would be something like a business trip and we all know that businessmen "never" have sex on those trips. And their wives "never" invite other men to fill the gap, while their husbands get their freak on during their business trip. It is very simple, people who want to be together work to find a way to do so. Every choice a couple makes in a relationship, either puts them closer to each other or further apart. Being with somebody is exactly what it means just being there in the flesh.

Now, I also want to bring your attention to something very important in our times, like romantic movies. While some of them truly try to be based in reality, majority of them are fictional and often impossible in real life. What is very important to understand, that all these movies end at a very specific point in the couple's relationship. Most of the romantic movies end on the man and woman getting together after conquering each other and every obstacle on their way. The ending of the movie is an apex of their romantic conquest. Telling the story of the couple any longer is dangerous; it might kick the romantic out of the story. Now they have to work to sustain their love against many dangers from the outside world. Life of a couple trying to afford their life, having kids and no sex, and finding out that living with another person could be difficult, don't make for a good romantic movie.

A high school couple that finally got together during senior prom in a romantic cataclysm, will have a 90% chance of breaking up when they go to different colleges in just few month. A low income couple, will find it hard to maintain their romance if they are struggling to pay rent and can't afford to see each other more often because they both work multiple jobs. A couple that talks on the Internet or on the phone for month and finally meets, will have many problems to overcome. Their first date is almost guaranteed to be disaster. What if they don't like how the other person looks or even smells? What if they kiss and they feel nothing and what if they have sex and don't like it even more? There is no way to salvage this situation. People need presence to make relationships work, that is why long distance relationships don't work, someone always ends up cheating or falling out of love. Or I would say this person is reacting to abnormal situation and real sexual needs by having sex with someone who is there near them. Regardless of what communication companies are telling you, we can never reach real intimacy by phone or email. You must be present in flesh and provide time for the other person.

There is nothing more romantic than young love on a sinking ship. A rich girl steals away few hours to have sex with a poor boy from a world way different than hers. And then what? In the real word, she would thank him for sex and bid him farewell. She would never give up the security of her rich existence, to forage for food in garbage cans with her lover. It just never happens. Even in many fairy tales, the poor man becomes a prince which makes it OK for a princess to marry him.

Yes, on the whole romantic movies are fun to watch if you understand that they are severely detached from reality or tell a story from the happiest part of couple's existence. These are fictional, embellished, and exaggerated stories are not based in reality and should not decide our day-to-day lives. Again, there is nothing wrong about caring deeply about another person. There is nothing wrong with giving gifts and planning activities the other person will enjoy. There is nothing wrong about having deep sensual sex with the person you care about and even role-play or experiment together.

But there is something incredibly wrong in taking fictional stories and measuring your life according to them. There is something very wrong in getting your unrealistic expectations from these stories, and punishing the world when it cannot deliver this impossible request. Reality can be very magical, if you truly live in it and understand it. Sometimes a single rose given from the heart is more meaningful than huge bouquet. Sometimes extra shift at work says I love you and care for you, more than a fancy gift. Real world has magic, but it is subtle. It could be waking up in the morning and saying, "I love you", it could be remembering your favorite food, and it can be as little as putting a band-aid on a cut finger.

And since, in our society "hopeless romantic" is almost synonymous with being an idiot, maybe the world ROMANCE should go away forever. We don't need a label for a feeling that is naturally in us. This feeling is what makes us want to make the world magical for people of whom we care the most.

And without a doubt we all want ***SEX***.

Absolutely nothing feels as good as sex. And if you don't believe it, (as the jokes goes) than you are not doing it right. If you are saying that you can live without sex, then you are lying to yourself or to everyone else. When two bodies are fused together in the agony of orgasm, it is a pleasure that can hardly be described in words. It is a transcendence of sort. It is like dying and being reborn at the same time:

"I will live in thy heart, die in thy lap, and be buried in thy eyes…" Benedick

Much Ado About Nothing by William Shakespeare

SEX doesn't need a fancy definition or a long philosophical

discussion of its true meaning. Every time we use our genitals for pleasure, alone or with another person, it is SEX. SEX gives us so much more than pleasure. SEX gives us confidence, emotional stability, a much deeper way to connect to each other, social acceptance, and babies. If you are still not convinced with tremendous importance of the word SEX, than I suggest a following fun experiment. Stand in the crowded room and scream as loudly as you can, just one word: "SEEEEEEEX". And see the whole room turn to you interested. Or while talking to friends at dinner or in the bar, say the word SEX and watch them pull in closer to listen. If you see the word SEX written in a title of the book, you will look inside. SEX makes for the best stories and juiciest gossips. Even this passage was made more interesting by this single world, sprinkled in every sentence. SEX is discussed and thought of constantly. And the act of it is so enjoyable, that it created both the oldest profession in the world and an industry that currently earns billions of dollars all over the world.

Unfortunately for us, we created a culture in which sex or wanting sex became dirty. We created a culture of denial where we all demonize one of the major joys of our lives. We took a basic need and made it into a sin. How did we do this to ourselves?

Let's face it; we get our morality from religion. I will bring up religion several times in this book, because it is such major part of our existence. And religion, especially western religion, dictates that sex is only for procreation. Having sex for fun or masturbating is considered a sin and waste of seed. Since all the major religions started in times where people lived in groups or clans, it is very easy to see why religion is pro-children. The more children you make the bigger your clan is. The bigger the clan, the more power it has against other clans. Now that we have abandoned the clan system, maybe we can drop the sex for "procreation only" premise. Besides, we like to have sex much more than we like to have children. Our urge to have sex and orgasms is much greater, than our ability to have children every single year. We cannot do it financially or physically in this day and age. I already mentioned previously how dangerous it is for women to have that many children, up to a point of dying.

Here is the mind fuck we are living in right now. Our bodies and minds tell us we love sex, while the morality we've been taught teaches us we only should have sex to make babies. This means that 95-99% of times we have sex, we feel guilty about doing it. We feel like we are pissing off God, which could possible mean Hell in afterlife. We are letting down our parents, our elders, and ourselves. These are huge suitcases of guilt that we drag with us every time we have sex. Now since it so natural to us, we will not stop having sex, so we always have to find way to silence the guilt, even if for one evening of joy. It is not easy to do, but we try. We try alcohol, weed, and other kinds of drugs. And they do muffle the sound of guilt in our minds and at the same time cloud our judgment. So when it is time to put on a condom we forget, or we just don't buy it ashamed of purchasing it in the store. Since our vision and mind is clouded, we sometimes don't notice our partner's obvious STD signs. Add to that lack of sexual education and you have a really serious problem. So when we get pregnant or sick we blame sex, while the right choice would be to blame guilt. Sex is not bad, unnatural guilt is bad. Just like there is a joy of being a good driver and a horror of being a bad, irresponsible or careless driver. There is a joy of being a responsible and safe sexual partner, but is it hard to do when you are trying to muffle thousands of years of guilt and repression.

For women guilt of having sex is even worse. There is a separate mind fuck that women have to go through. As I established previously, in an Alpha male society women are treated as property. And for a "property" their value is closely linked to virginity. If a woman looses virginity, she depreciates in value. There is even jokes that compare loosing virginity and uncorking a bottle wine. There and incredible pressure not to loose the "magical hymen" until the "right" man comes along. This tiny membrane causes women lots of guilt and anguish. So women are expected to know very little about sex and stay virgins until the magic fellow on the white horse arrives. Here is where mind fuck comes in. Men like women experienced in sex or at least interested in different ways to please their men. Yet, because of religious guilt men would scorn and condemn women who are interested in sex, making them feel dirty and marginalized by society.

It is terrible crime to not educate people about sex and trying to scorn them for consequences of not knowing. Often these consequences like STDs and pregnancies are used as a reason against sexual freedom. **SNEAKY ADVOCATES AGAINST SEX TRY TO EQUATE SEXUAL ILLITERACY AND STUPIDITY WITH SEXUAL FREEDOM. FREEDOM WITHOUT KNOWLEDGE IS DANGEROUS AND SO IS SEX WITHOUT KNOWLEDGE. KNOWLEDGE IS POWER AND TRUE FREEDOM.**

So, we as a society, have a very strange, unnatural, and self-destructing relationship with our sex lives. SEX is natural and keeping it in the dark is unnatural and dangerous. So, let's bring sex into the light, where it belongs.

No better place to start than **PORNOGRAPHY**. Here is a whole industry that recognized our yarning for sex in our suppressed world. First time I ever learned anything about sex was in pornography. There was no manual for 13-year-old boys called "You and your Penis". There were no classes in school covering sex or even puberty. When I got to high school, there

45

was no class to teach me anything about my growing need. Parents didn't discuss sex with me, fearing I will just start fucking and forget about college. In fact, all I knew about sex is that it was a taboo, dirty thing that adults did. All I knew were rumors that my friends heard and some movies, which faded to black after pre-coital kiss. It was presumed to be super fun and a complete mystery to my friends and me. When it became very clear that I want something from women and it was called sex, my teachers looked at me from TV. Pornography was a mind-blowing experience in my teens. The abundance of beautiful naked, sexual women was unbelievable. Their sexual honesty was refreshing and the sexual positions they used were amazing. Yes, after watching my first porno film, I wanted to do it. More accurately, I already wanted to do it, but now I wanted to do it right. Pornography didn't answer my questions about feelings or STDs, but it did show me that sex exists. At the very least, I learned the basics like man suppose on top and woman on the bottom, which is the glorious missionary position. Coincidently, it is a position only humans, chimps, and bonobos practice. We are so lucky to have this position, which brings maximum intimacy of being face to face with your partner. Pornography *literally* showed me what I have to do with a woman in my bed. At least I learned that my erections and my need to jerk off were not evil. More so, I learned that I wasn't the only one in the world interested in sex.

The oxymoron of our society accepts girls being inexperienced in sex, but man are expected to know what they are doing. Yet, nobody teaches man how to do anything. Now the kids are a bit luckier in that sense. Sexual Education in one form or another is slowly making its way into our schools. Internet has provided answers to many questions that come up. Still there is a whole lot that needs to be done. And I will talk some more about sex education through this chapter. For now I want to acknowledge, the importance of pornography for doing three very important services. Once again, it makes sex a joyful celebration of life. Second, it makes it a universal activity, uniting us all regardless of our differences. Thirdly, without a doubt the visual representation is priceless in the lack of any other out there.

For all of you, who think that pornography is bad: Pornography is a service. Like any industry it will not exist if there was no need for it. And the industry that makes around 8 to 10 billion, in US alone, fills a serious need in the market. Like any industry this size, it tries to challenge and innovate. Sometimes they innovate to a degree, that some people find uncomfortable. Yet we must remember that sexual preferences and desires are a taste and what is Heaven for one could be Hell for another person. Also remember that no alternative to pornography exists, just loads of shame and denial. Pornography teaches us the physical aspect of sex. Nobody else does.

So we should come out of the closet and admit that we like porn. We like watching beautiful people in the act of sex, which is a form of art our human brain deeply enjoys. We are great mimics, and love mimicking what we see on the screen. Pornography is also not new. It existed in one way or another for thousands of years. Whether it was cave paintings of naked breasts or statues of naked man in women. Whether it was paintings, photographs, or films we were always interested in naked human form.

And if Pornography is not new, **PROSTITUTION** bares the title of the "oldest profession in the world". Just think of what this means. Word 'profession' implies a better than average skill in the art of making people cum. Also the same word implies that it is a job that satisfies a real need in the market. Word 'oldest' implies that it was a first real trade a person can go into and claim proficiency in what he or she does. Now it is well understood that this trade is dominated by women at a rate of 90%/10% or even 95%/5%. This is just a cultural and biological bias. Men are unable to fake arousal. Like in poker we are either all in or we are out. No amount of lubrication can undo what our eyes see as not fuckable. And nobody says that it can never be 50%/50% someday or it might even go away some day. For now we have to see it as reflection of the need in the sexual market. And there is a real need out there. Why?

The answer lies in many aspects of our live. For one, men are biologically geared towards spreading their seed to as many women as possible. This is an evolutionary mechanism that once put our humanity on the map in large numbers. It sounds like a good excuse, but any species that can reproduce in large numbers can have a better chance of survival. To have lots of babies both male and female members of the species have to have an enormous sex drive. The evolutionary drive to impregnate as many women a possible is in every man on Earth. In the beginning of human history this drive had no restrain. And only beginning with 20th century, men try to control it to preserve their monogamous relationships. For women, the sexual drive pushes them to try as many male partners as possible. This is an evolutionary system that allows a woman to choose the best possible mate, thus to insure the best possible offspring. So our promiscuous nature is always there as a way to propagate our species. Now, this sexual drive is widely considered a problem or at very least a nuisance. There is an enormous societal pressure on both sexes to control the sexual drive. Still there are very big differences between what is expected from both sexes.

Half of our society consists of men, who are full of semen and sexual desire. Men are encouraged by society to have lots of sex and praised for being promiscuous and having lots of sexual partners. Male life is all about food and sex. Men obtain money and success only to obtain better food and better sex. Men on the average want sex more often, because evolution requires them to be eager and ready to propagate the species. Again it is not an excuse, just a fact of our existence. Male need for sex is so great that it gave birth to brothels and strip clubs. Erotic dancing was always around and was always a great way to get men exited and ready for sex. Modern day strip clubs live on a promise of sex, with no sex delivered at the end. A man walks into the club to be bombarded with naked bodies and stripped of his cash. Yet, unless it is a seedy club, he has to walk his desire and erection outside with no satisfaction. Men are not even aloud to touch the women, but the strip club is such a joyful celebration of sex, nakedness, and flirtation that they are still around. Promise of sex is such a strong emotion that it is even a part of a business model. Countless restaurants pack themselves with sexy waitresses and hostesses. Countless stores have beautiful female employees, whose presence guarantees patronage of horny males. Mind you, none of these places sell sex. The promise of sex is enough for exploding male libido. So, we definitely have an enormous need for sex on the male end of the equation.

On the other hand, women are constantly pressed by society to be sexually restrained. It is a fact, that women want sex just as much as men. They get much more out of it, like multiple orgasms. (As a joke goes: When your ear itches and you scratch it with a finger. What feels better the ear or the finger?) Unfortunately society made women into keepers of monogamy and surrounded them with shame and guilt, dwarfing their natural desires. A woman is expected to be inexperienced in sex and have no interest in learning about sex. Any woman who is experienced is considered low class or dirty by our society. We are all raised to hate our naked bodies, but women have extra shame imposed on showing their naked flash. Add to that religion that constantly demands covering bodies including the face and demands sex only to make children. Add to that the fact, that female orgasms were not considered a necessity or were even considered nonexistent for thousands of years. You have a society where majority of women enter their sex lives not knowing what to do, or even how to have a normal one, or what is expected from them.

We have another oxymoron on our hands. Men with heightened sexual expectations and free pass from society; and women with repressed sexual desires and expectations, and a society that values their virginity above them. This creates an enormous gap between male sexual need and what majority of women can provide. Prostitution fills this gap, providing both experience and everlasting readiness to please. I don't think I will be far off in saying, that a good number of men experienced the best sex or a blowjob with a prostitute. I am sure women would love to fill this gap for their men, and many do very successfully. Still, the societal pressure to be virgins and sexually closeted is so great, that it leaves both sexes feeling cheated and lost. Most men would find it exceptional if their wives or girlfriends were more sexual. Yet these same men would condemn these women for being sexually free. If this is not a mind fuck, I don't know what is. As a result both sexes miss out on a lot of great, normal, passionate, and creative sex.

Until we realize the strain we are putting on our sex life, prostitution will flourish filling the gap in our lives. On a smaller scale, prostitution provides much needed sexual experience to those people who society chose as unfuckable. For few dollars, these people can feel desirable and experience the joy of an orgasm. Sounds almost like charity, but it does make prostitution the most tolerant profession in the world. We have to understand that for now it is not going anywhere and embrace its existence.

And it is very important to embrace the prostitution as part of our society and finally legalize it everywhere in the world.

Those of you who refuse to acknowledge it as part of our lives are living in the state of denial. One argument against prostitution being legal is that wrecks homes or lets men astray. This is a smoke and mirror argument that I already answered above. We have created this oxymoron situation and blame ourselves for not being able to live in it. And this is just a sad fact that it takes prostitution to shed light on the fact that our society ignores the real needs of men and women. Another very important point to mention here is that nothing happens out of the blue or by itself. **WE ALL, MEN AND WOMEN, MUST WORK HARD ON BEING SEXUALLY INTERESTING TO OUR SEX PARTNERS.** Speaking as a man, I can say that no man will shell out money on a prostitute if he has good sex at home. Second argument states that legal prostitution will mean that people will do it more and use prostitutes more. Really? For me this argument is a hard sell. Now it is illegal in majority of places in this world. Yet, you scratch the surface of any city and you see an endless barrage of brothels, "massage" parlors, strip clubs, and dark corners filled with streetwalkers. All of them are chancing being caught by police and facing serious consequences if it happens. Their customers risk being caught and exposed and having their life possibly ruined, including loosing jobs and families. Yet it still happens a lot to the tune of billions of dollars. If laws and cops can't stop people from being people, legalization of prostitution will hardly matter to the rate at which we have sex. And third and final argument claims that prostitution breeds STDs and AIDS. Of course it does, because we left it in the seedy underground. Who screens prostitutes and their customers for diseases? Nobody! Do they follow any safety standards? There are no standards! It is forced to be a seedy, criminal enterprise. It is like throwing a chocolate bar into the dirt and then blaming the bar for being dirty.

Legalization of prostitution is a must for many reasons. First, it will pay taxes. Imagine sex making money for our country's budget. Every time you cum, Uncle Sam will get a dime. Imagine your citizen's pride in knowing that orgasms help building schools, roads, bridges, and pays for your retirement and health care. Believe me, prostitution will be very impressive revenue for the government surpassing marijuana, alcohol, and cigarettes. Second, legal prostitution makes it a legal business that has to abide by laws and regulations. This means always using condoms, customers of agreed upon legal age, and above all STD and AIDS screening. Both customers and prostitutes would have to satisfy a disease free evaluation before participating in sex. Imagine, crime rates will drop, STDs and AIDS will drop, and we possibly would be able to balance the budget too. All of this for legalizing something we do a lot anyway. There are even examples that prove that it will work. In 2003 Rhode Island District Court decriminalized indoor prostitution. As a result, from 2004 to 2009, there was 31% decrease (824 fewer cases) in rape offenses and 39% (1,035) decrease in cases of female gonorrhea. Also in 2014, at the 20th International AIDS Conference in Melbourne, researchers presented a very important study of sex workers in Canada, India and Kenya. The study concluded that decriminalization of sex work can reduce HIV infections in those countries by 33 to 46%.

Our moral enlightenment will take sometime. We might grow into a society, which treats sex as grownups. We might in the future embrace our sex life to be open and universally enjoyable. For now we might take sex out of dark corners and make it disease and shame free.

It is also very important to notice, that both Pornography

and Prostitution acknowledge a universal truth in our lives.
WE CONSIDER A BEAUTIFUL BODY A GREAT ACHIEVEMENT.

While beautiful face is mainly luck, a beautiful body requires work. We all know how much effort it takes to make our bodies worthy of praise. People we consider good looking get away with many things other people cannot, almost if beauty is the key to happiness. Personally I would say that beauty and the brain together is better, but you can get by on beauty alone much either than on brain alone. We enjoy when beautiful people talk, eat, walk, make love to us. We even enjoy them having sex with another beautiful person, aka pornography. Regardless of our advanced brain, we are visual creatures and we like visual stimuli.

Some things we deemed universally bad like bad odor or being fat. Bad odor is a sign of low hygiene and could be a sign of disease, either way it is a huge deterrent for us. Extra weight looks so unappealing, that is literally number one daily concern for everybody. Conversely, a great sent can be like a drug for people. We all enjoy immensely smelling baby heads and we love smelling people we are sexually attracted to. We like people with good bodies so much that we dress them like dolls and marvel at them. We even made it into a very coveted profession, showering them with money and calling them supermodels.

We are so visual that there are some attributes we consider universally important. A major one is pretty face. We stare into each other faces the whole day and a pretty face is very pleasing to us. What we find very appealing is unblemished skin, clear eyes, intact teeth, luxuriant hair, and kind expression on the face. It is a very clever evolutionary compass. People with clear eyes, intact teeth, and flawless skin are usually devoid of the diseases that would ruin these features. It is a way to choose a biologically stronger mates, to produce a stronger species. Our face is a wonderful reflection of state in which we find our health. Most of our inner health problems find a way to be reflected on our face as uneven skin, bloodshot eyes, or yellow routing teeth. Beautiful faces appeal to us and usually the main thing we consider. Above all, a great smile can make the face the most appealing to us. And when this smile comes with dimples, it is even more appealing. One of our favorite sayings is "smile and the world smiles with you". Or we like to say that the best make up for a woman's face is a smile. Smile is the most welcoming thing we can do to another human being.

There are some other things we find attractive that are more gender specific. On women they are large breasts, low waist-to-hip ratio, big expressive eyes. For men, it is usually broad shoulders, deep voice, strong chin, and being tall.

There are some universal factors that boost our appeal no matter how we look. For men it is always good job and money. Every woman wants a man who could be a good provider. Even though, nowadays one income family is becoming a myth or just impossibility. Men are still expected to bring money and provide for family. And even though most of the women work, they are still expected to cook and clean well, raise the children, and still have time to sexually please their husbands. A woman's wet dream is a millionaire with a big penis. A male wet dream is a sexually curious woman with amazing cooking skills.

There are other features out there that we find attractive, but at the end of the day it is very personal. We are all a sum of our upbringing, environment, personal experiences that completely shape our view of the world, what we want from it, and it even shapes our faces and our physique. Sometimes we know whom we want just by looking at the person. Sometimes it is decided by a first kiss or a first conversation. And sometimes it decided by a first time we have sex.

And when we do have sex are we safe? Do we know what safe sex is? Do we even know the basics?

We live in a world which seriously lacking in sex education. Yet, after food, sex is the most enjoyable and coveted part of our lives. It is not only responsible for our main source of pleasure, but it is also responsible for our species survival and success. Why then we learn in school about retarded kings and their endless wars, politicians and their corrupt dealings? Why do we learn and memorize writings that have outdated themselves and just pollute our minds? And why we learn almost nothing about our sexuality, when it so infinitely important?

Everything we do, working out and attaining money and success, is to have a good satisfying sex life. And we are thrown in this world knowing nothing of sex or even some of the basic hygiene. And then when we fail to have sex safely or successfully we blame sex itself for being a curse on our existence. We even try to do something as stupid as Abstinence-only education to stop people from having sex before marriage. In United States alone we spend close to 200 million dollars a year for Abstinence-only education, despite the statistical evidence that it doesn't work. A strong sex drive is an evolutionary mechanism that made our species so numerous and successful. It cannot and should not be stopped. Poor teens are bombarded with sex in movies, on TV, in books and at the same time are told that they must stay away from it. It is impossible to do! Every person who had an orgasm knows that there is no feeling like it in the world. And to live without this feeling, of dying and being reborn in orgasm, is impossible. We should not blame sex for our lack of knowledge; we don't do it with anything else. If a first time driver crushes a car into a fence, we don't blame the car we blame the driver. Once the driver learns to drive the car safely, he or she can get the maximum joy from driving. Just like driving, cooking, skiing, swimming, and everything else we do, safe sex requires learning and lots of practice. Over the years some brave people have created videos and books detailing safe and enjoyable sex practices and I can't cover it all. We must have sex education in school. ***PREFERABLY, I WOULD START TEACHING KIDS IN PRE-PUBERTY AND INTO ADULTHOOD. FURTHERMORE, I WOULD START WITH HYGIENE CLASS AND ADD GRADUALLY SEX EDUCATION CLASS RIGHT BEFORE PUBERTY.*** Both classes would be serious, with exams and serious care about providing honest and impartial education. Imagine in a future, a guy will ask a girl to have sex and she says: "Hell no, you failed your Hygiene and Sexed class!" Or someone will ask to have sex without a condom and will be told: "Hell no. First you haven't been tested yet. Second, it is irresponsible to ask to have unprotected sex in a casual relationship with uncertain future. And third, it is irresponsible to ask without having financial means to raise a child." ***IMAGINE A FUTURE IN WHICH WELL-EDUCATED ADULTS WILL MAKE SAFE AND RESPONSIBLE CHOICES IN THEIR LIVES!***

For now, here is a quick and basic discussion of safe sex, which I hope will help people now.

First, I want to talk about contraception. ***WOMEN CARRY BABIES IN THEIR BODIES, SUFFER HORMONAL JUMPS, SUFFER BODY CHANGES, HAVE CAREER DECISIONS THAT COME UP WITH PREGNANCY, AND HAVE TO FACE EXTREME POSSIBILITY OF HAVING TO RAISE THE CHILD ALL BY THEMSELVES. SO NOBODY, BUT WOMEN HAS THE RIGHT TO DECIDE ON BECOMING PREGNANT.*** Most of the time, numerous children are not a dream come true, but more of a nightmare for women. Thus contraception and condoms are not new and have been around for thousands of years. Women in the Roman Empire used an herb called Sliphium. It was so successful and used so much, that the Romans drove it into extinction. Receptacles made of linen were used in Ancient Egypt as predecessors of modern condoms. You must have children only if you are comfortable with the idea and use contraception when you are not. By no means you should deny yourself pleasure of sex, but you can deny unwanted consequences.

Since we are living in a 21st century and with AIDS as part of our lives, every long term sexual relationship should begin with mutual blood work testing for AIDS, Hepatitis, and other STDs. Having this assurance will make sex better, more fun, and more adventurous on the oral side of it. Anyone who says, "Trust me, I have no diseases" is either uninformed, idiot, or a liar. A lot of medical conditions are dormant in the blood or show no visible signs on a person, so blood test is a very prudent and honest thing to do. I think it is a great way to tell your steady partner I love you and I want you to be safe.

It also helps minimizing your sexual partners. It is always great to have one sexual partner and have as much fun with that person as possible, but it is not always the case. And monogamy doesn't have to be the answer to safe sex. No matter how enjoyable it could be, casual sex is always more risky. The less you know about your sexual partner, the less you know about his or her sexual history. Sometimes an extra date or conversation can reveal a lot more about prospective sex partner.

Another very common sexual mistake comes from the shame we have about our bodies and sex in general. Majority of sex happens with the lights out and not looking directly at genitals that are about to be fused together. Also majority of sex happens under influence of drugs and alcohol. Both either obscure or impair your judgment. When you are drunk or stoned other people might seem better than what you actually see. You have a good chance to forget to put on a condom or put it on incorrectly. Also having sex in a well-lit area gives you a chance to examine your partner for visible problems, like genital sores and rashes. You can check your partner for discharge or unusual odors. Having sex with lights on is more intimate and a great way to get more turned on by your partner's naked body.

Here are some more great tips to make your sex play safer:

● ALWAYS USE CONDOMS with unknown sex partner for all forms of sex, vaginal, oral, or anal.

● ALWAYS USE ORAL DAM, SHEER GLYDE DAM, or DENTAL DAM for vaginal oral sex.

● Always put condoms on sex toys.

● Always use a glove for anal and vaginal penetration.

● IF IT HURTS YOU, STOP! This applies to oral, vaginal, or anal.

● NEVER DO ANYTHING THAT YOU DON'T WANT TO DO!

● Always use ONLY WATER-BASED LUBRICANT. Never use oil-based lubricants like petroleum jelly, baby oil, cooking oil or lotion. Oil-based lubricants weaken the latex, causing breaks.

● Spermicidal Nonoxynol-9 is not recommended because it can irritate vaginal and anal tissue.

This brings me to my favorite form of contraception the glorious, ever available, ever reliable **CONDOMS**. My whole life they get bum rap from people and "experts". Many women and men claim that they feel nothing with condoms on. And, while "experts" and many women, let me down through the years, condoms never did. As a man I can honestly say that sex does feel better without a condom, but it is a luxury that you can only have with a steady partner. And even then, you don't want to get your partner pregnant every year. So, condoms are a small sacrifice in sensation, but have many other advantages. One advantage is that it doesn't require women to use daily hormonal pills. Second, it is very reliable when used properly. And third, they could be used as part of foreplay.

Condoms have been around for thousands of years in one form or the other. Originally they were very expensive and only available to the rich and noble classes. In ancient Egypt men used linen sheath, in Japan they used leather or tortoiseshell sheaths. In China they used silk or lamb intestines. In 1500s linen sheath soaked in chemicals was used against syphilis epidemic in Europe. While in 1800s condoms where made famous by Giacomo Casanova, who used them frequently and successfully. His promiscuous life style was a great credit to condom efficiency. He used to inflate them to check for leaks prior to use, as an original form of quality check. During his lifetime condoms where made from sheep intestine treated with sulfur or lye, with a ribbon to tie them around scrotum. They also started to be sold in brothels to general public. In 1839 Charles Goodyear invented rubber vulcanization, and in 1855 first rubber condom was produced.

Unfortunately, many moralists through the years prevented condoms from being used widely. They were demonized as unholy or just evil or a cause of promiscuous behavior. One example of such overzealous ignorance came up in World War I. The British and American soldiers were the only ones to whom government didn't provide condoms, but instead introduced a "chastity campaign" to force soldiers into not having sex. As always while trying to stop something natural, the result was a disaster. 150,000 British soldiers, while stationed in France, were admitted to the hospital with venereal disease. Almost 400,000 American soldiers were diagnosed with syphilis or gonorrhea. These statistics were so devastating that they finally gave condoms recognition and popularity they deserved.

Unapologetic Manifesto

In all fairness, condoms did have historical failures, but mainly from improper use or having no standards of production. Poor people, because of them being expensive, sometimes reused linen condoms. First latex condoms did leak and were not always reliable. Currently, latex condoms are well tested and have to comply with certain standards, which are enforced by agencies like Food and Drug Administration (FDA). They come well lubricated, in different shapes, sizes, colors, and even tastes. Condoms can even be cut to make into a dental dam for oral sex.

Condoms still require a responsible user to use them consistently and only with water based lubricant. It sounds silly as a reminder, but you must use condoms throughout the entire sex act. Never take them off before you are done. Another silly and scary reminder, that condoms must be unrolled on an erect penis. You have to pinch the tip of the condom before unrolling it to leave the reservoir tip for your sperm and unroll it all the way to the base. And after ejaculation, you must grip the condom by the rim and carefully withdraw it. Gently pull it of the penis, without spilling sperm and place it in the garbage right away. Finally, keep the condoms in a cool dry place and always check expiration dates before use.

Safe sex requires preparation. It's a responsibility of both sexes. Keeping fresh batch of condoms by your bed is a great start. Buying condoms that fit your male companion better is even more responsible. Depending on your lifestyle, you might want to think of some mobile options. If you like to have sex in weird, dangerous, and public places, you need to make sure you have condoms there too. Still, there is nothing lonelier than a condom inside the man's valet. Valet condoms can get pierced, worn out, and are a gloomy reminder of the male teenage optimism. I suggest using a tin or plastic condom box. It would be great to keep one in the car. I personally put two condoms in my pocket before any big night of drinking and partying, just to make sure I don't do anything stupid. If given a choice, my personality favors a cozy bedroom, where I can explore every inch of my lover in peace. Bedroom is the safest place for sex, but I am all for exploring new places to pleasure each other. No matter where you do it just remember to protect yourself from unwanted pregnancies and pesky venereal diseases.

If used properly condoms are very effective. A June 2005 Study of "The Effect of Correct and Consistent Condom Use on Chlamydial and Gonococcal Infection among urban adolescents" have shown in favor of condoms. It concluded that correct and consistent use of condoms resulted in 90% reduction in the risk of gonorrhea and a 60% reduction in the risk of Chlamydia. In 2005 according to USAID, when used correctly and consistently condoms are 90% effective in reducing HIV transmission. And, according to www.Plannedparenthood.org, perfect use of condoms makes them 98% effective against pregnancy. Even if not perfectly used, condoms are still 82% effective against pregnancy.

And if all I said, didn't convince you to use condoms. There is only one safe mode of sex that remains. You are certainly very familiar with it from your puberty and those delightful dry spells. Masturbation is safest form of sex, when performed in a safe and religion free space. There is no downside to masturbation. It makes you learn about your body. It releases tension and makes you happier when orgasm causes the release of endorphins, dopamine and oxytocin. It even helps to relieve body aches and menstrual pain. It helps to keep your body sexual between partners. And it just feels great, because nobody knows how to make you cum better than you.

As the matter of fact masturbation is part of my favorite medical story from the 19th century.

Unapologetic Manifesto

It is hard to believe, but up until 20th century American and European men believed that women didn't have orgasms, sexual desire or pleasure. So when women, devoid of orgasms, complained of anxiety, sleeplessness, irritability, nervousness, it was thought to be a disease. Added to that was feeling of heaviness and erotic fantasies. The doctors dubbed this "disease" as "Female Hysteria". And the treatment was amazing. Doctors and midwifes would apply vegetable oil to women's genitals and massaged them with two fingers inside and a palm on clitoris. These poor "patients" had orgasms and miraculously were cured until the next appointment. Understanding of women and their needs was so bad that their orgasms were called "paraxysms", since women were suppose to be incapable of orgasms. Imagine doting husbands taking their wives to regular doctor's visits just so the doctor can make their wives cum. This treatment was so popular and so exhausting for doctors, that doctors were responsible for rise of vibrators. "Poor" doctors overwhelmed with demand complained of fatigue and cramping. These doctors used vibrators to make their customers cum faster in matter of minutes, as compared to 30-40 minute sessions. And kids, that's how vibrators were born. Yet this sad and hilarious story has important point, masturbation and sex are very healthy for human body and mind. They make a world of difference for us.

There are many benefits of sex. Good sex gives our pelvic muscles a good workout. Orgasms cause contractions, strengthening the pelvic muscles. A study in the Journal of the American Medical Associates even showed that men that have more than 21 ejaculations per month are less likely to have prostate cancer. People who have frequent sex have more immunoglobulin A (IgA) and thus a better immune system. There even studies out there which show oral sex being very beneficial for women. Specifically, swallowing semen can protect women from pre-eclampsia (onset of high blood pressure during pregnancy). After sex hormone Prolactin is released that is responsible for making us relaxed and sleepy. I don't know of a better sleep aid than sex, certainly beats taking pills. And if all this is not enough for you, sex can make you smarter. Study on the middle-aged rats in the University of Maryland concluded sexual activity improves mental performance and increases neurogenesis (production of new neurons) in hippocampus (a region of the brain responsible for formation of memories).

Isn't this enough of reasons to get going as soon as possible? Didn't I give you enough reasons to get addicted to sex? Of all the addictions out there sex is the healthiest one for us, when done safely and thoughtfully. There should never be a disease named "Sex addict", only one called "Stupidity Addict" or "Ignorance Addict". Sex made our species great. Human penis is one of the best, if not the best specimen of male genitalia in the animal kingdom and for a good reason. Better penis makes for better sex and thus makes us have more sex and babies. We had enough of being ashamed of our sexual bodies. We had enough of being ashamed our natural, lustful desires. We put ourselves in the chains that suffocate us and make us insane. We must break the chains and embrace sexual freedom as a normal and happy way of life.

After all, great sex can only bring you closer to that magical, illusive word **LOVE**.

Love is a very interesting word to define, precisely because we cannot come up with a definition that makes everyone happy. We define love in the dictionary as deep affection, strong personal liking, or attraction based on sexual desire. I like the last definition for acknowledging importance of sex in the process of falling in love. Another reason for confusion with love is the fact that we have many kinds of love.

Unapologetic Manifesto

For the sake of this discourse I will only deal with romantic love. I will not deal with love of parents, children, siblings, neighbors, country or God. These loves are often fake. They are fake by nature of being obligatory. This is the kind of love we confess to the most and mean only 20% of the time. It is only fair to mention that obligatory love only feels real to us after the object of love has proven to be worthy. This emotion is rarely explosive and all consuming. Obligatory love can grow on us with time, but it will never consume our lives like the romantic love does. Bottom line, if your parents, friends and countrymen wrong you, you will give up on loving them. You will choose to not love them and some times even hate them. Another thing that makes obligatory love special, is that it is the only kind of love we can understand. It grows on us slowly and we logically choose to accept it in our lives. We can provide exact reason for this love, be it money, mutual respect, common interests or years of shared joys and disappointments. Unfortunately, obligatory love doesn't get to the core of us, as does the romantic love. It doesn't have the ability to break us or give us wings, because it is a logically calculated decision.

Strangely, we don't know what makes us fall in love on our own? We accept a stranger into our lives and we make this stranger a recipient of the strongest emotion we can feel! Why it is one person and not the other? Why do we let this emotion consume our lives and defy logic and self-preservation? Why does it change? Why it sometimes a person we least expect? And finally why can't we rise above this emotion? Why can't we logically remove it from interaction with each other?

In my opinion, the reason people are unable to define love is because they see it as a single stage process. Everything happens at once and grows bigger or lesser with time. We see it as something that happens out of the blue, to the lucky ones. It is very evident in the expressions we use like "love happens", "we FALL in love", "fairy tales can come true", "love strikes again". Our symbol for love is cupid. What is cupid, really? A naked baby angel, thus with a childish mind, who hunts for people with his bow and arrow. He shoots us unexpectedly based on his whim and we are left to deal with consequences. And we go on "love struck", "love slave", "smitten by love", "we fall head over heels". All these terms indicate no control or a decision on our part. It is just something that happens to us and something that we have to deal with for better or worse. We even go further than that. Since we often fall in love with a wrong person, we often see love as a curse or a disease. And we come up with expression like "lovesick", "starry-eyed", even "enchanted" indicating even a magical power that love holds over us.

No matter what expression we use, it is obvious that we are clueless about love. As much as we want it, we are also very much afraid of it. For us love is a hostile take over that will either make us or break us.

To me love exists in two stages: involuntary and voluntary. The involuntary stage happens first and most importantly never stops. We see a person and we feel a strong sexual attraction to them. Let's not fool ourselves about the true nature of the attraction. The person we see is a stranger and we have nothing else to go by, but their looks. The sexual attraction is very important. The person doesn't have to be the best looking person in the world, but sexually they must be able to rock our world. It could be their face, eyes, smile, dimples, and their hair. It could be their physique or even the shape of their toes or fingers that can grab us. It could be their perfume or natural body smell. It could be the way they talk or the sound of their voice. It could be combinations of all above-mentioned things that make us feel sexually excited about the person. Either way, having sex

Unapologetic Manifesto

with this person feels like something we really want. This person usually will give us mind-blowing orgasms, which we will never forget and which never happened with other people. More so, we want this orgasm repeated over and over again. We want to smell and touch this magical person again and again. He or she will be our best and scariest addiction and we feel it very deeply. The sexual and visual satisfaction they give us is very intense and sometimes (not very often) irreplaceable. This is the first an involuntary stage of our being in love process. Personally, I think it is more than 50% of the process. I think sexual attraction and quality of orgasms are responsible for almost 70% of why we love someone so deeply.

The second stage happens when this person opens up his or her mouth and starts doing what they normally do. At this stage whatever the person says and does can either deepen the feeling of attraction or put a serious doubt in our minds. If we find kinship, friendship, laughter, respect, and understanding then the feeling will deepen. If we find indifference, selfishness, sadness, fear, or even danger we will start to fade away from the person. And we will even give 50-70% of our sexual attraction, if the other person will disappoint us so much. Of course, it is so hard to give up that some people stay for years with a wrong person.

When you have a great stage 1 with great satisfying sex and a great stage 2 with great friendship and laughter you are set. Of course in real life it is hard to line up both things with good percentages. The combinations are endless, but I can say with certainty that sex below 50% will be a major reason for falling out of love. Unfortunately, in our world it is not just love that keeps people together. We are also having governments, which are strangely interested in our sex lives and who we stay with and who we leave.

This brings us to the holy "institution of **MARRIAGE**".

To begin, it is one of the driest expressions to describe something as emotionally charged as marriage. That aside, the word "institution" brings with itself a whole lot of baggage. If you think about anything that calls itself an institution, it is an entity with specific rules and standards. Rules and standards imply reward and punishment systems. It is also understood that these rules are written by a group of people, they are not appearing from thin air. So what we have is an "institution of marriage" that is created and controlled by people and the rules these people agreed on. It is a very narrow, even suffocating window, through which we adults have to fit in order to fit in with the rest of the controlling group. There is also something very scary about these rules; they imply very rigid standards of what is right and what is wrong between two consenting, sexual adults. And of course you might say that standards are important to keep people in line, and to some degree it is correct. Society strives on rules that keep it going forward and away from total anarchy. The problem comes in when rules become inflexible or the standards of right and wrong are not updated with increasing intelligence and newer knowledge. At the very least, we have to understand that whatever was "working" even 100 years ago, is no longer the case.

We have to boldly admit that marriage is an antiquated system and let it go once and for all. Marriage exists now and being widely defended for a lot of wrong reasons, but it suites the governments and religion to keep it place. Marriage works very well to keep population in its place as well as shift the financial responsibility from government to the family unit. Imagine each family as a clan; sure they are different in size and other attributes from clan families of the past. They are still similar in basics. If you don't believe it, just remember what happens when two people get married. Their two very different families come together and are forced to share their lives. For anyone who observed this process, knows that is like two universes crushing together. Sometimes, the differences in clans are so numerous and irreconcilable that it causes the couple to break up. In fact, what really happens is a weaker family being swallowed by a stronger one. This is how different and set in its ways families are. Each family has specific rules and traditions that **MUST** be followed. Each family holds itself accountable for finances and mistakes of its members and feels that it is in constant competition with other families. So if a family member messes up, the family steps in to help and government loves not having this responsibility. Families distribute wealth, morality and health care. We really don't have citizens, and just microcosms that act like small governments and oppress their tiny citizenships. Families are even responsible for education of its members, and dogmatizing these members for life. Families educate each member in their narrow view of the world, very often passing their misconceptions and prejudices to their children. It takes children years and separation from family to be exposed to new or different ideas, which often would make them family outcasts if adopted. Instinctively we know that such isolation from the rest of the world is wrong, which makes another popular saying a tell-tell sign. "It takes a village to raise kids" is very popular saying and it is absolutely true. Of course, many people would say that it takes a number of people to successfully raise a child and that is all it means. I would change this saying slightly to "it takes a village of ideas to raise a normal human being". Again, the family unit is such a tight environment, that new ideas might be very hard to come by. Another very important downfall of family, you can only be as successful in life as the financial means of your family will allow. Sure there are rare exceptions, but your opportunities are severely limited by your family. You can even argue that your upward mobility and ability to get a better job is either dwarfed or accelerated by your family. Either way, we are not working with a leveled playing field. For many of us, our future is decided by which family we were born in. I joked with people for years on this subject. Every time someone asked me why I wasn't rich, I would tell him or her that I crawled out of the wrong vagina and that was the reason.

Our world partitioned severely into families fighting against other families. Thus family unit, like any closed group, is one of the major obstacles preventing us from having unified world.

Yes families are a real money saver for the government, which normally would have to take responsibility for the health and education of its citizens. Government spends an enormous amount of energy to enforce marriage. We have tax laws that track and provide minute benefits to married couples. We have courts that make sure no marriage is left lightly and is practiced according to the rules. Even after divorce government keeps the couple in a phantom financial marriage, not to be burdened with kids of divorce. Government even reserves the legal authority to say who can marry whom. That is a weird power that government doesn't really need to have, and which gay community fought for years. Personally I think no one should stop anybody from getting married, because it is a very nasty way of telling people whom they can sleep with. It is also a way to take away social rights from those people government deems undesirable.

It is very important to remember that we are all told to find that ONE special person to make all our dreams come to true. This is an enormously stressful search, which has to end with us committing to the relationship for life. And once you make it official you have to make it official with two entities Religious Institution and Government. Now both of them are tracking your marriage with serious bias. While religion makes it a union of souls in the presence of sometimes-merciful God, it implies that this Union is for life. Religion implies that this bond for life, an unbreakable bond. Sure you can try to get out of it, but there are serious financial consequences and peer pressure. First, your religious peers will try to talk you out of breaking the bond, since it is considered a major sin. One can argue, that misery likes company and they don't want to be miserable alone. Even if your peers have nice intentions and think that they are saving you from Hell, they have no right to assume that what you are currently living in is not Hell already. And then your religious leaders will spend numerous hours trying to convince you against your divorce, testing your resolve. Finally, if your resolve is strong you will have to go through a ceremony, which will cost you money, and then the merciful God will set you free. Still, you will remain with a label of "divorcée" among your peers, and will be treated like having an affliction of some sort.

At the same time, government makes it a social contract between two people. Like any contract, it can be broken, but with some very serious social and financial consequences. On social level it might require you to redo your name and passport, if you are a woman. Both men and women, have to change living arrangements, very often change banking venues, social circles and just about every part of their life. When kids are involved, battling parents inflict a serious mental damage on the kids, which makes them torn between the two people they love the most. For both parts, the financial consequences are very serious. We are living in society where it is very prudent and necessary to have a two-income family, so divorce brings both parties near financial ruin or even makes them seriously destitute.

There is enormous amount of money that is made on marriage from start to unfortunate or fortunate finish. Restaurants, wedding planners, match makers, family lawyers, family counselors, family courts, government officials in various branches all rely on marriage for their income. Whether marriage succeeds or fails somebody is making a lot of money of that. And 50% of marriages do fail according to many statistics, which you are welcome to search out on line. This 50% are the marriages that were so unhappy that they dared their financial strength to come out of them. These are 50% of brave souls who decided not to live miserable anymore. But what about the remaining 50% are those solid marriages? I think it is safe to assume it is not a solid number. Let's say modestly that another 10% gave up on trying and changing their reality or accepted unhappy marriage and just marching happily to their death. Let's assume another 10% are scared to divorce because of political, financial, social and religious reasons, but still are very unhappy. This would make roughly 70% of marriages are failing, or marriage has only a 30% success rate at best. And if something is failing ¾ of the time, it is not a successful system at all.

Of course, arguing about marriage is arguing two issues at once. And I will gladly cover both arguments since they have been on our minds for ages.

The first argument is polygamy verses monogamy. This is a very tough issue to tackle since I personally believe in polygamy, yet I know that I will not be able to handle it emotionally. I am, like all of you reading this book, is a product of my upbringing. I believe in being faithful to my mate and would 100% expect the same from her. I take my marriage very seriously and will not consider anybody else but my wife. (And no, she didn't tell me to write this) It is not easy to accept a world were people don't need to commit to one another. I think it takes a serious emotional enlightenment to bring humanity back to a polygamous people we once were. It might take few generations and culture changes to see us as one people marching into the future. It will take us time to realize that some chains we broke, were worth breaking. It is interesting to note that our ancestors, while polygamous in nature, still had mates they preferred and stayed with always. I assume it was an unspoken bond that reached much further then fidelity, but more an amalgam of joint sexual and life experiences or just simple joy of familiar and simple survival. Either way, they were committed to some member of the group, while they remained absolutely polygamous in nature. Even in ancient Rome orgies were a regular thing, yet it didn't interfere even a little bit with people getting married and staying committed to a single spouse.

Right now, we are somewhat far from understanding the dangers of monogamy or how we are really not designed for it. Even the way we view polygamy is skewed. When we imagine polygamy we don't see it as an equal opportunity employer. All we see is a man having sex with many different women and keeping them as wives on call. We don't see it in its true sense as a two way street, both sexes being allowed multiple partners. Even worse, we ONLY see it as sexual process. There is much more to polygamy than sex, it introduces a much higher potential for diversity and going outside your tiny suffocating group. Religion coupled with extreme nationalism keeps us locked in our groups. This keeps our gene pool stagnant and prevents it from diversifying. In a sense, we are dwarfing our own evolution. In fact, polygamous species has a better chance of survival and this is what we were. This is what made us so great and so numerous. It is a very serious and very important game of genes, in which we as species cannot afford to loose.

Any species on Earth is sort of like a virus with another bunch of viruses fighting against it for survival. This one virus must constantly fight and diversify in order to stay current and survive. Humans as a species or a virus need to constantly diversify its gene pool for survival. This is called *Heterozygote Advantage*. This is a process by which genes of two parents create a child, which is a hybrid of both gene pools and is fitter and better version than the parents. It helps to think of genes as a blueprint that carries essential information to make a person. The blueprint has information on immunity, the codes for physiological and psychological advantages and disadvantages. It carries all evolutionary advances made including size of the brain, imprinted instincts and responses.

Now remember that there are virus and other threats in the universe working against our survival. They are constantly diversifying and expanding posing a bigger threat to us. We must constantly evolve to stay competitive with our enemies. If we don't and our gene pool becomes stagnant, we will become weak, vulnerable, and with time extinct. One of my favorites is **Red Queen Hypothesis**. Explained very crudely, it states that we as a species must work really hard to evolve just to stay in the same place. The same place being competitive and protected against the threats that are trying to eradicate us. Imagine us and the viruses, that are trying to kill us, running side by side. It's a race. They are constantly diversifying and becoming better at killing us. We also must constantly diversify and become better at protecting against them and killing them. Constantly refreshing and strengthening our gene pool is the only way to win the race. Diversifying gene pool requires men and women from different parts of the world coming together. It literally requires them to *cum* together. Polygamous species, unbound by social prejudices will have the best chance to diversify their gene pool.

Both men and women will find multiple people as attractive in their lifetime. Men are designed to spread their seed by putting it in as many partners as possible. Females are designed to search through multiple males and choose the ones with better gene pool to impregnate them. There are even interesting studies that try to prove our polygamous nature, even if controversial, they are still very thought provoking. One such study was printed in 2003 in the magazine *Evolution and Human Behavior*. It is called "The human penis as a semen displacement device". The study looks at the age-old question of why male penis has such a bulbous head? Why is it shaped like a mushroom? And no, it is not so your hand will not slip off, while you are jerking off. The study actually claims that the head of male penis is designed to pump the sperm of a rival male from the female reproductive tract. Another way of saying this, a female has sex with multiple males and only the one with better penis will get her pregnant. Imagine a woman having sex with five men in a row. All of them are ejaculating into her, shooting for that golden egg at the end of the fallopian tube. According to study the head of the male penis (coronal ridge) creates suction during thrusting that draws foreign semen away from the cervix and clears path for own semen delivery. If you imagine it, this process does sound as a real possibility. I can see a penis in a snug vagina pumping away and with each pump the other semen runs over the bulbous head, over the ridge and away from the cervix. In this situation, a man with a bigger penis and bigger coronal ridge would displace the rival's semen and impregnate the woman with his juice. And a bigger penis is an evolutionary advantageous trait, even if some men refuse to admit it. I am personally only 70% sold on the argument of this study, because nothing in the world is that simple. You have to figure the shape of the cervix in question, motility of the sperm, sperm count and quality of female egg in question. Even with all these variables, it is a very compelling argument for human penis looking as it is. I would add, that since we are now very well aware of the G Spot, maybe the coronal ridge had a purpose for that too. Humans are almost exclusive in having sex in a missionary position. Now with a woman on her back her G spot is on the top of vagina, so it is possible that a large coronal ridge was an evolutionary advance to hit G spot in the missionary position.

Another study published in the magazine of *Evolutionary Psychological Science* in June 2015, looked at the quality of male sperm. The study concluded that when men are exposed to a new female, the volume of the sperm increases. Also there is an increase in sperm motility and sperm count. And the male subjects ejaculate quicker, as if they can't wait to impregnate the new female they got exposed to. All of these pointing again to the fact, that men are designed to impregnate as many **different** females as possible and not one woman specifically. It is an evolutionary design to spread male seed, not something men plan on purpose. It is also another compelling argument for polygamy.

I also understand, that when we are talking about polygamy in general it is not the same thing as diversity. Yet, our current religious and monogamous society is such a serious threat to diversity, which we so desperately need for survival of our species. We don't even need to insist on polygamy in the name of diversity. All we have to do is stop preaching monogamy as a norm. Each person has to have the right to choose if he or she wants to live a monogamous or polygamous lifestyle. And we must stop punishing people culturally and financially if they stray away from being monogamous. ***TRUE FREEDOM LIES IN MAKING YOUR OWN CHOICE IN MATES.***

Our body is very well designed to seek out diversity. I think it is about time we started to listen to our bodies instead of misleading ideas that other people impose on us. As the matter of fact there is a chemical that does this job for us and helps us to feel attracted to a mate with better and more diverse genes. I think this chemical is so important, that you cannot call yourself and adult without knowing at least something about it.

I am talking about wonderful, magical, and absolutely

indispensable *MHC (Major Histocompatibility Complex)*.

You can write a whole book discussing importance of MHC. Simply put, MHC is a gene cluster coding for cell-surface proteins that helps our immune cells distinguish our own cells from invaders or antigens. MHC helps T-cells distinguish between own and antigen cells and that is very important in our body's defense against outside threats. MHC spans every cell in our body. Most important for this discussion is that MHC is in our skin cells, saliva, sweat, mucus, tears. Also it is very important to know that people have unique MHC, making each of us a snowflake with its own defense coding.

Evolutionary process guides us in a direction of diversifying our MHC. This means that we are always looking for mates with MHC different from ours, so the resulting offspring will have a better more advanced MHC defense mechanism. Thus, the species gets better survival when different MHCs come together. Since MHC spans every cell it acts as guide in us choosing our mates. MHC present is saliva is responsible for taste. MHC present in Pheromones is responsible for a specific smell. **A PERSON WHO HAS MHC, WHICH IS DIFFERENT FROM OURS, SMELLS AND TASTES BETTER TO US, AND WE ARE ATTRACTED TO THIS PERSON SEXUALLY.** For years I was a firm believer that a kiss can tell you much more about how much you like the person, than even a conversation could. And now I have my proof in MHC. Now you know why every relationship begins with a kiss. It is like an evolutionary handshake to determine the correct mate.

Women prefer the smell of men, whose MHC genes are significantly different from theirs. Men use MHC as well to choose women they find desirable. We all have our roles to play, still I would argue that a choice woman makes is more serious and more involved. Women bare the enormous responsibility to bare children and that makes their choices deeper. Of course, just because woman chooses a man it doesn't mean he will reciprocate in kind. I do believe men are more open to suggestions and have a better flexibility in choosing mates. Still men can get off their high horse and admit that it is women that chose men not the other way around. This doesn't make me less of a man; just a man who understands how evolution works. At the end of the day, woman chooses a man with whom she wants to make kids and continue our species. All MHC does is help her to make the right choice.

When a woman becomes pregnant her body doesn't need to search for mate anymore and her MHC preference reverses with hormonal changes that occur inside her body. So pregnant women prefer men with similar MHC, which could explain some sexual problems couples have during pregnancy. Consider this, when women take birth control pills it fools their body into thinking it is pregnant and reverses the MHC preference. *SO IT IS THEORETICALLY POSSIBLE THAT WOMEN ON BIRTH CONTROL PILLS ARE POTENTIALLY LOOKING FOR A WRONG MATE WITH SIMILAR MHC AND MIGHT BE VERY DISAPPOINTED IN THEIR CHOICE ONCE THEY STOP THE PILL.* Could it be that it is responsible for misguiding the main defense mechanism that we have as people? And if it is true, what then? For all those men and women, who insist that pill is better than a condom. Maybe it is time to think that small rubber barrier is better than being stuck with a wrong person. It is not only your happiness on the line here, but a survival of the whole human race.

Right now, we are always cautious in practicing **EXOGAMY**. This is a practice of going outside the group and trying something new. I would even say that Exogamy is more important than Polygamy for our survival. If you practice

Exogamy and stay open to the people outside of your group, you will be surprised at all the interesting and rewarding experiences you will have. As long as you practice Exogamy you have a better chance of finding the right mate, and it will not matter if you choose to be polygamous or monogamous. Exogamy gives diversity a chance and a chance for you to be happy. There are many signs out there that always point to advantages of diversity. We always marvel at children from mixed race couples, admiring their beauty. We are not always presented with evidence that is not just skin deep. We study important things very poorly sometimes, but there is evidence out there for diversity. The journal *Nature* published a large genetic study of 350,000 individuals in 100 different countries. The study showed that the more distantly related an individual's parents were the taller and smarter they tend to be. Four traits were seriously improved with genetic diversity of their parents: height, lung capacity, general cognitive ability, and educational attainment. Just add to that better immune system thanks to MHC, and you will realize how awesome diversity is. It is like making a new superhuman with each generation.

Now the second part of the marriage argument is government control of population's sex life through marriage laws. Is it needed or unneeded? Is it too much or just right? This is another complex issue that gets debated a lot.

To be honest, a label "MARRIED" doesn't add anything to relationship at all. It is a very empty word, like all words are. It doesn't make you love harder, have better sex, have children, and it doesn't guarantee happiness. It is purely a social label used by our society and as such it has a number of disadvantages and advantages. It only matters on social and financial level, not between two consenting adults in love. "MARRIED" is a social contract, which is as scary as any contract can be. It is a contract we make on our own free will, yet not always able to understand the consequences and hidden meaning in it. We also not always mentally prepared for such a contract, but society pushes us to sign it anyway. Like any contract, not understanding it doesn't save you from being punished by it.

We also must come clean on how we REALLY feel about marriage. We should not be confused by how we told we should feel about marriage by our religious and government leaders. The real us always shine through our jokes and our words. I was always a big fan of jokes and enjoyed their honesty about our existence. As the matter of fact, jokes get funnier as they get closer and closer to our true reality. So what do we joke about when we joke about marriage? We joke about cheating spouses a lot. We joke about having lousy married sex a lot. We joke about being sick and tired of each other after a long marriage a lot. We joke about ungrateful kids that ruined our lives a lot. And we joke about being married and having no money also a lot. I really have not heard any jokes that make married life sound better than single life. There are even jokes about murdering your spouse. This is a very bleak spectrum of jokes on a subject of marriage. Is this how we really feel? Yes we do. And we feel guilty for having these feelings, like we've been taught to feel guilty about all are natural feelings.

Our words give us away even more. They scream at us that we really see marriage as social and financial trap and we see it as terminal as dying. Some words we use bluntly equalize getting married and dying. Look at these awful words we use like "tying a knot", "taking the plunge", "you play, you pay", "buying the cow", "hooking up the ball and chain". We also call marriage "license to fuck", "beginning of an end", "settle down", "getting hitched", "life-sentence", "another one bites the dust". Some of these phrases are very chauvinistic; some are very bleak and hopeless. Some thesauruses even have a word "mistake" as synonym for marriage. We truly think that marriage is the end of life. I can give you the biggest prove there is. It is called a Bachelor or Bachelorette Party. It is a very odd way to celebrate your happiness, by saying good-bye to the single life, while groping naked strangers and drinking yourself into a coma. Why do we need this party at all? Well, because we think that life ends on marriage. This is incredibly sad. If you feel that you absolutely NEED a bachelor party, you shouldn't get married at all.

I saved my favorite word for last, "wedlock". It is a very telling word because of the word lock, which in my opinion has two separate meanings. First meaning goes along with regular rhetoric that marriage locks you in a position from which it is hard or impossible to get out. It locks you for life or till death do your part. Second meaning is locking up happiness, which we all crave. We feel happy, sexually satisfied, and even blissful and we want this feeling to last forever. We take photographs and videos, but they are not enough. They are just frozen moments of happiness. Locking the person to us seems like a way to have a never-ending happiness, but we fool ourselves like that. Then we get disappointed and crush even harder. **LIFE IS A FLUID, ALWAYS CHANGING PROCESS AND WE MUST ACCEPT CHANGE AS PART OF LIFE.** Nothing, including us, is forever. People who do better in life are people who accept that life always changes. You get knocked down and you pick yourself up. Both sad and happy cannot be constant. They alternate or go in blocks, but they always switch. Accepting changes is a way to grow and stay current with the times. Once even computers were a big change and those who embraced changes were rewarded with better jobs and better understanding of their reality.

Between the jokes and the words, it is a miracle people

marry in such numbers. I think that majority though do it to please God, who considers marriage very sacred and divorce a sin. Or we do it because we have been taught that an apex of any successful relationship is marriage. While government interest in marriage is purely financial.

So should the government be involved in marriage? Yes and no. When it comes to whom you want to marry or have sex with government has no right to interfere with that. Government can't forbid any kind of love, sexual expression, or sexual pairing. The only time government can say that certain sex is forbidden, if this sex is a cause of a plague on human race. If having sex with goats killed a person by giving him a deadly disease and it could be spread to others, then the government can go on TV and say, "Please don't fuck goats". Pedophilia is one area where government has a right and moral obligation to call it a crime and forbid it. **OTHERWISE, GOVERNMENT HAS NO RIGHT TO PASS JUDGMENT ON YOUR SEX LIFE OR YOUR CHOICE OF SEXUAL PARTNERS. GOVERNMENT HAS NO RIGHT TO PENALIZE YOU FOR LEAVING OR TELL YOU WHOM TO STAY WITH. WHAT TWO CONSENTING ADULTS DO IS THEIR BUSINESS.**

When it comes to the consenting adults having kids, it seems that government should have the right to set some rules. Even though every new citizen makes the community stronger, he or she is also a financial strain on the economy and on the resources like food and water. It is a very delicate issue and shouldn't be tackled lightly, but when you think of a well being for the whole community government might need to interfere. And the only real purpose there is to balance the existing resources with the existing number of citizens, not to single out people and forbid them to have kids. Even when government decides to make rules on having kids, it will be a 100% bad idea. You can never pick and choose, who will have kids. There is no right way to decide this. For example, an intelligent individual might want the government to decide that having kids should be only for people with high IQ. Yet, a person with a low IQ might carry and important gene for immunity and the gene will be lost with IQ rule. And the lost immunity gene might have been a solution for a virus that we might not find again. Someone else might come up with another rule that will regulate who is born and again it will be extremely wrong and dangerous. When it comes to our growing population, government should only concentrate on the plan that will find purpose and place for new citizens. One thing that always comes to mind is colonization of other planets and space travel. The real truth is that you cannot force citizens to be responsible or conscientious when it comes to societal needs. You can only educate them, not trick them, into right choices. When a citizen has a decent place in a societal structure, he or she feels like their needs being met and purpose provided. This kind of a citizen is motivated to keep his or her position in a society by making responsible choices. Government keeps Marriage Laws only to force citizens into being responsible, but since it makes them miserable Marriage Laws should go away.

At the very least we all can agree that people should be allowed to get a marriage license at a certain age. If we need a certain degree of understanding and development to drive a car, we should need similar rules for a marriage license. And I would say even 20 years old is too young for a marriage license. Car rental companies consider anybody before age of 25 a risky customer and I always wondered how it came about. The answer lies in the development of the human brain. I don't know if car rental companies did their research, but as far as I am concerned the answer is in the brain. Limbic Region of the Brain develops by the age of 15, which intensifies our emotions and makes us take more risks. It also pushes us to be more with our peers and less with family. It is like our brain is trying to put us inside this world and make explore the life outside our family. It seems almost as an exciting adventure, but it is horrific when it is left unbalanced. The Prefrontal Cortex in our brain is responsible for sound judgment and impulse control, but it develops only by the age of 25. So from development of the Limbic Region to the full development of the Prefrontal Cortex we have 10 years during which our impulses and emotions run almost unchecked. This seems like an easy period for someone to get in trouble. So if until age 25 we are too risky for car rental, we should be also too risky for city hall. So if we cannot dispense with marriage as unnecessary label, can we at least make it available only at a later age? I propose that individual must be at least 25 years old to get a marriage license.

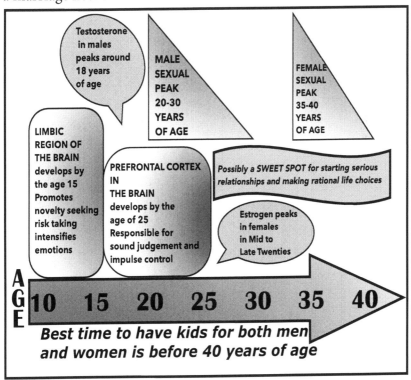

Unapologetic Manifesto

I have designed this graphic representation of our development from age 10 to age 40, so it easier to see these important years for what they are. Maybe seeing it like this will give us some ideas of how to make our lives better and help us understand why we act certain way. Maybe it will help in guiding us into responsible choices, which improve our lives instead of crushing them.

Overall there are three reasons for this whole enormous chapter. One reason was to uncover the tremendous hypocrisy between what is and what we are taught to believe and follow. We are sometimes presented with "reality" which is so bad, that it takes years and a number of serious mistakes to understand how false this "reality" is. The second reason was very simple. **ALL I WANTED TO DO IS TO SHOW THAT BEING WITH SOMEBODY HAS NO LABELS.** Even worse, sometimes it is even beyond our reasoning or rational understanding. It could be a person's smile, sense of humor, the sparkle in their eyes, their beauty, the beauty of their intellect, or simply the way this person makes us orgasm over and over again. And this is just right. This is how nature intended us to be. As we discussed before, we have plenty of help in MHC to choose the right mates. And I made mates plural for a reason. Through our lives we will meet a number of people and there will be more than one person that will ring our bell. I don't say we have to find them all, but we certainly don't need to hold on to the ones who are toxic for us. If you came to understanding that the person you are with crushing your dreams, leaves your sexual needs unattended, and refuses to build a future of mutual happiness, THIS PERSON HAS TO GO. Our lives are too short and too tough to be wasted in agony of being surrounded by wrong people.

And finally, the third reason has to do with sexual freedom. It was something we always had from birth and now almost gave up completely. Our sexuality is so repressed by religion and numerous groups that think they know us better than our bodies do. It seems that almost everyone around you has an opinion on how he or she wants you to live and who to live with. **SEXUAL FREEDOM IS A BIRTHRIGHT. AND IT IS ABSOLUTELY NOT SYNONYMOUS WITH SEXUAL STUPIDITY AND BEING IRRESPONSIBLE ADULT.** Having unprotected sex with strangers is stupid in the age of AIDS and numerous STDs. Having sex or babies for a wrong reason, just to lock people to you for life, is stupid. It never works and hurts you even more than loosing the person. Having lots of children, when you don't want raise them, can't afford them, is just irresponsible. It is irresponsible as an adult, as a citizen, and as a parent who will punish his kids just for being born. Freedom with accountability and responsibility is what makes up a successful society. Freedom without those two things is just anarchy free-for-all chaos.

It is funny, but I always wondered why we are so fascinated with some celebrities and gangsters. They are mostly selfish, in majority of cases devoid of morals and responsibilities. They are really tough to admire, yet there are numerous shows, books, movies, newspapers, and blogs that cover their lives. Why? Well, they are the only ones in our society who openly exercise the freedom of being above the rules we are all following. They can be above government or religious laws. They are very free and unapologetic in their sexual choices. They throw money at us and we leave them alone. Or we leave them alone because it is fascinating to see someone coast above the rules. Eventually, we want to see them fall. We want them to crush, so we know that no one can be above the societal law. Still, we do spend a lot of time reading about them exercising their sexual freedom and their sexual stupidity. In fact, we seriously admire those celebrities who exercise their sexual freedom, while remaining responsible adults and citizens. The ones who exercise sexual stupidities are the ones we keep for entertainment and to help us reaffirm our closeted existence. Overall, we feel burdened by seemingly endless number of rules we put on ourselves. We built our own cage and now the bars and the tight space are suffocating us. All we need now is courage to break free.

We all yarn to safely exercise our sexual freedom, to love, to be loved, and to have a purpose. We all yarn to drop labels that bind us, judge us, and guide us against our nature. We are not broken or evil. We are just scared, misdirected, lied to, and we simply lost our way. Otherwise, we are beautiful, resourceful, daring and worthy of a better future. **THIS FUTURE IS POSSIBLE, BUT NONE OF US CAN ACHIEVE IT ALONE. IT IS SOMETHING WE NEED TO ACHIEVE TOGETHER TO BE TRULY HAPPY.**

Oleg Bershad

The oxymoron of loneliness in the age of communication.

As I sit down to write this chapter I have to admit that I almost didn't write it at all. My original plan never included a chapter on loneliness. Now I realize that this is going to be one of the most important chapters I will ever write.

It is very hard to understand the true meaning of loneliness, unless you felt it yourself. It is a very universal and the most self-destructing emotion that we have to overcome. Everyone has it and everyone must find a way to deal with it. It doesn't matter what you do it is always there. You can be a part of a big loving family and you will still feel lonely. You can be a great businessman drowning in millions and still feel lonely and misunderstood. You can be a member of a group and still feel lonely in a group surrounded by many other people. Loneliness has many shapes or forms and it is responsible for many mistakes we make in this world. Our misunderstanding of loneliness is a problem in itself. How is it possible? How can you share a bed with someone and feel lonely? Has the universe, in all its wisdom, left an unfillable void within our hearts?

We experience loneliness first time as children when we

miss our mother, while we are alone in the crib. After that we experience loneliness every time we are in bed alone at night. We are forced to stay alone and in darkness and in silence. Our thoughts are left to be our only entertainment, but we are very clear about what we think about. It is always about the events of the previous day and mentally punishing any wrong doing that comes to mind. It is always wondering about future, your abilities, your desires and your hopes. You always wonder, will I make something of my life? Will I wake up tomorrow? Is there a future for me in this world? Will he or she stay? This is our loneliness! We have nobody to say it will be all much better. We have to face the giant world alone and carve out a small bit of happiness for ourselves.

If you still not clear about loneliness, turn off your TV. Silence. You are alone in your room. There is nothing to distract you from your thoughts. How does it feel? What thought comes to your mind first? Do you think of others or always about yourself? Do your problems come and line up in front of you? Do you have to deal with them, finally? Do you realize that you are mortal and this is not forever? Do you search for meaning in your life? It is clarity and fear, yet it is an amazing way to get your scattered thoughts together. It is a way to slow down and listen to your mind that was trying to scream above the sound of TV, computer, and your phone. We are so sped up and overwhelmed with information, we are not practicing slowing down. The only proper way to examine your life is to slow down and try to listen to what the world is telling you. Of course, temporary state of loneliness is not loneliness. It is silence. And silence is important for us from time to time to gain clarity and understanding. Constant silence is loneliness and it is definitely not the state we all desire. An individual is said to have a balanced life when he can combine silence and group activities without feeling overwhelmed or lonely. It is very hard to do and something we all must strive to be.

Century after century we try and fail in our attempts to get rid of loneliness. Even our planet is like a lonely spec of dust that floats among many uninhabitable planets that are nothing like it. Worst of all, as we evolve more and more as people we get more and more lonely. In the age of electronic communication with Internet, planes, and satellites connecting us, we shouldn't be so lonely. Instead we are growing more and more apart from each other. The technology, that was meant to connect us, is just giving us a way to escape any personal interactions.

I see teenagers ride on the train together to school. Five or six of them make plans to meet and ride together. Yet each of them sits looking at his or hers phone, completely immersed into this wonder with flickering lights. They don't talk to each other the whole ride. Maybe this makes me sound elderly to the young generation, but this kind of get-together seems pointless. Why meet at all if you are only talking to your phone? What is the point of six isolated islands riding together? Electronics will never replace the need to talk and to touch. And two emojis having sex is not the same as having sex with another human being. We have to understand that as technology goes forward, our minds have to advance as well. If the technology is more advanced than our brain can handle, it is a big problem.

IT IS AN INTELLECTUAL PROBLEM. WE UNDERSTAND THE WORLD WE LIVE IN SO WELL THAT WE ONLY CAN COME TO ONE CONCLUSION: WE ARE FOREVER LIVING IN GROUPS AND EACH SINGLE ONE OF US IS ETERNALLY LONELY.

The first thing to understand is that we never feel one kind of lonely. There is loneliness we feel when we are without a partner in this world. This is an intimate and the most difficult loneliness we feel. Then there is a second kind of loneliness it is directed to the rest of the world. It is when we say to ourselves I am alone in this world, group, city or universe. We have to address both kinds of loneliness. Even though they both have a similar solution.

I strongly feel that the key to a solution lies in one word: **PURPOSE**.

Lets deal with first kind of lonely. It begins with us trying to understand ourselves. What do we want from and for our future partner in life? Most of us ask this question quiet often in our search for a mate. Yet we are very seldom asking ourselves this question: What will our future mate want and expect from us? Or to dive even deeper into the problem, we seldom ask ourselves what do we need to improve in ourselves to get a desired mate. A great relationship is give and take and we can't expect to take all the time. This especially rings true when you look at your life and see that you attract same kind of people or make same mistakes over and over again. Something has to change in you at this point. You have to change yours looks (and I don't mean plastic surgery), your personality has to be adjusted, and your expectations must match the real world. Your life must have some kind of plan, which includes a mate and career. Both parts will have to get an equal share of the pie that is your supreme attention and presence. And most importantly you must realize that nobody is happy alone, just like no one is happy being with a wrong person.

So you choose a **PURPOSE** for your search and don't let loneliness compromise that. The soul sucking pain of being alone should not let you settle for someone who will be totally wrong for you. It is not better to be with someone and miserable than lonely. By the way, having kids doesn't take away the lonely; it only creates an illusion of lost loneliness by making you very busy. As wonderful as kids are, by no means they are a substitute for a healthy adult relationship, which includes conversation, sex, and emotional and physical support. Many people claim to be too busy to be lonely and they can go on for years singing this tune. How often do you hear, "I am too busy with work or kids to be lonely or to date?" The scary truth is that work and kids will go on without you. It might not be the same, but life goes on and eventually they will not need you as much or at all. What will you do then? Will you crush face first into the wall of loneliness or will you make a pathetic attempt to find another distraction? People need people to share laughter, sorrow, and sex. People need people to share the joy of achievements and help soothe the sorrow of disappointment. People need people, and most of the time of people they are sexually attracted to, to feel that their life is complete and not lonesome. There is no substitute for a healthy sexual life for an adult. Sex is a way to connect to your partner. Sex is emotional therapy. Also, speaking from a personal experience, only meaningful and deeply felt sex takes away the lonely. If you find a person with whom you have meaningful sex and you care for each other, then you are lucky. Next step is to have a joint purpose in life. There must be a goal towards which you are both working together. It could be anything that makes both of you happy. It could be getting a house to call it your home, it could be having lots of kids together, it could be buying a restaurant and running it together, and it could be all of the above.

Think of a relationship as a carriage with two horses. Inside the carriage is the weight of our existence. We put everything there our work, chores, personal and social problems, kids, relatives, friends, bills, hopes and dreams. You and your mate are running together pushing the carriage along the path of life. It was a very heavy carriage to pull by yourself, and it feels lighter when you pull it together. You work your asses off during the day, but at night you disconnect the carriage. At night it is your time to love to hold each other and to have your carriage-free time. Imagine now, that each of you has a different purpose or different direction to go to. You can't agree on the same direction, but you decide to go for it anyway. You pull and you pull, but the carriage doesn't move. You get frustrated and angry at each other. You blame each other for the carriage not moving, even though each of you pushes with a maximum effort. You will eventually start thinking that you will get to your destination faster if you split the carriage in two and go in your separate directions. And kids, this is what we call a divorce in our times. Only with a joint purpose or a joint direction the carriage can move forward in life. It is supremely true for loving couples and our society as a whole.

HAVING A MEANINGFUL, GIVING SEX LIFE AND JOINT PURPOSE MIGHT BE A KEY TO A HAPPY LONELY-FREE LIFE.

The second kind of lonely we feel is much broader in scope. Still it is very important kind of lonely, because most of the time it is responsible for 50-60% of loneliness we feel. Our society has grown to such a size that it is very easy to feel left out. It is very easy to feel to feel like you don't matter at all. Corporations make us feel like numbers on the page and replaceable. Governments make us feel abused, lied to, unimportant, or a burden. Our voices seem to drown in our giant, divided, bickering mess of humanity. **AT THIS TIME HUMAN RACE HAS NO JOINT PURPOSE, NO JOINT CAUSE, AND NO JOINT GOAL TO UNITE US ALL.** That leaves us empty, searching for even a tiny group that will give us a chance to feel as part of something much greater than ourselves.

Our need to belong is overwhelming. We need to know that we are much more than mortal flash. We need to know that our lives are not just food and sex (as great as they are). We need to feel that we have a place in this world where we are always welcome. We want to be a part of a group that shares our ideas, hopes, and dreams. To be a part of such group seems magical to us. We search for these groups all the time and many websites, societies, companies, religions, cults, and businesses make beautiful money facilitating these connections. It is so important for us to see familiar faces and being able to feel safe and protected. On a larger scale, we really need a cause much greater than ourselves to fill the empty void inside us. And if we don't have a cause or purpose of our own, we search desperately for someone with a purpose or a cause we can join. The bigger the purpose the better it is for us. All it means that there is a bigger group of people you can call "sisters" or "brothers". You can go to the meetings to share food, alcohol, and the amazing joy of being a part of the same cause. You can meet on the streets and high-five each other for wearing the same T-shirt, chain, or even the same hat. For our brain it is absolutely necessary to be a part of a cause that makes us more important than just a middleman between the kitchen and the bathroom. Purpose is the most powerful drug our brain can be on. It so pleasing, overwhelming, uplifting and soothing, that we live it everyday and in every breath.

Professional sports figured out our need to belong very well and they try to make every fan feel like part of the team. You want a team jersey? You got it. You want to pretend you are playing the game yourself? You got it. Here is a video game for you. You want to watch the game with thousand of people, who love the game as much as you do? You got it. Here is a stadium for you to watch the game together. We will even sell you food and beer to make it more fun. Want to form a deeper bond with fellow fans? Here are some season tickets, fantasy game clubs, and sports bars. This is all wonderful and great fun, until team rivalry kicks in or it becomes an ugly, bloody war where people fight for their teams.   Yet, it is a purpose that somewhat fills people's lives.

When it comes to purposes and causes, no paddler of purpose is more successful than religion. Our overwhelming need to have a purpose and belong is the number one reason religion is strong in the world. Can you imagine that there is a God who created you and the universe? And can you imagine that you can be part of "Team God"? And can you imagine that God deeply cares about you and has a purpose for you? Wow, that is great cause to join. And *your* "Team God" is an international team with millions of members all over the world. You can have "your" people everywhere and you can even recognize each other by gold chains or clothes you wear. You don't need to feel lonely no matter where you go. Even after you die, you will be with "your" people in Heaven and you don't need to be lonely there either. And your benefits don't stop there. Religion promises that all the hardships you endured on Earth will be compensated by eternal bliss in Heaven. Wow, indeed!

Believing in God took the anguish of living from many people. Religion even served as a keeper and purveyor of basic morality. It even housed scholars and gave them the ability, opportunity, and place in which they can pursue their scholastic studies. Overall, religion was very successful in providing purpose to many generations. And as anything that worked well before, religion is now outdated and realistically needs to go away or seriously acquire a new direction for itself.

RELIGION:

Don't Believe The HYPE!

Not talking about religion is like ignoring an elephant in your living room. Here is the elephant taking up 80 % of space, but no one is talking about him. Out of fear or lack of information, no one dares to speak. Everyone feels the presence of the elephant and everyone feels the pressure of limited oxygen and space in the room. We all feel his breath behind our backs, yet no one dares to talk about getting rid of the elephant. If only we could remove him from the room, imagine all the oxygen and space we would get. Instead, we feed the elephant and help him grow. We do our best to breath the remaining oxygen and squeeze our growing population into the shrinking 20% of the room. Nothing good will happen if we will stay silent. We will be squeezed out of the room slowly and disappear into nothingness. Nothing really gets done unless we start talking about it and let the conversation push us to the right solution. ***EVERY ASPECT OF OUR LIVES MUST BE OPEN FOR RATIONAL CONVERSATION.***

Unapologetic Manifesto

So lets have a rational conversation about religion.

To start, I am not a hater or a judgmental person. I am not a democrat or republican and I don't wish to be associated with either party. I simply don't want to be locked into a narrow ideology of any group. I always try to listen and to understand people around me, because it is a right and moral thing to do. Only by listening and understanding the other people's views you can truly know who they are. Only listening to other people you can see how similar we all are. You can see that we all need similar things from our lives. Being set in one way and not listening sets you up to see the world as "us and them". This path only breeds hate and destruction on us. **HATE BREEDS HATE**. And is hard as it is sometimes, we must learn to love our humanity and understand that everyone is born with a clean slate. We become who we are from multiple interactions with our world and what we see through the small window we get into this world. Internet helped us a lot. It made the window to our humanity much bigger and more accessible. Now it is time to use our knowledge and our brainpower to make the world into place we always dreamed of. We want the world in which love breeds love. We want the world where love, understanding and knowledge completely eradicated bigotry, hate, and ignorance.

When I wrote this chapter on religion my goal was not to criticize or start with a rigid stand. I totally understand that millions of people found their purpose and emotional comfort in religion. My goal is to start a serious conversation. I want to ask questions that I think are important and hopefully will make you think of how we should move forward as citizens of Earth. First and most important, we are human race and we are citizens of planet Earth. Everything else exists above that on the surface. We are all members of the human race and we are all living on this unique planet, which is what makes us similar and united. Unfortunately, we have a very long history of not being able to stay united. When you look at religion, there are way to many religious practices out there to threaten our unity. **WITHOUT EVEN DOING ANY SERIOUS STATISTICAL STUDY, WE ALL KNOW THE FIVE MAJOR RELIGIONS: CHRISTIANITY, ISLAM, BUDDHISM, HINDUISM, AND JUDAISM.** Aside from these five major ones, there are thousands of variations, spiritual traditions and groups. Each groups has its own ideology, way of dressing, way of living, way of cooking food, even a way of getting married and having sex. To me it seems like way too much of division to introduce into our existence. It also important to understand that under most religious tradition, doing things differently is considered a very big sin. Some religions even claim that believing in something different makes the other group dumber and even less human. Preaching that difference is a sin, is preaching hate. And we know that hate only breeds more hate, more misunderstanding, more fear, and more divisiveness into the world that is already in pieces. Christianity alone has over 30,000 variations, while believing in the same basic principles. Pilgrims came to North America, because their Puritan view of Christianity was not acceptable to English Church. They crossed the ocean in a tiny boat, risking certain death, because of religious prosecution. We can talk volumes about Inquisition and Crusades using religion to openly justify ethnic cleansing and genocide. We can talk about modern, more subtle ways religious prosecution have been responsible for millions of people killed for their differences in worship. I will not do that. Instead I have a simple question:

THERE IS ONE EARTH AND SUPPOSEDLY ONE GOD. WHY DO WE NEED SO MANY RELIGIONS? WHY DO WE NEED THOUSANDS OF WAYS TO BELIEVE IN ONE ENTITY?

Unapologetic Manifesto

It is my understanding that the purpose of religion is to introduce morality, humility, and understanding into our world. Aside from worshiping the creator and giving us eternal peace, religion has to be an agent of bringing us closer to each other, not further apart. Then why till day this there has not been a "One Earth, One God Convention"? Why, in the name of brotherly love and peace on Earth, have all religions found a way to come together? It only seems logical, to settle the differences and create one single way to worship God or one universal religion. It is not a simple task to embark on. Erasing so many years of separation and hate is hard. Still, as a religious leader you should feel a moral obligation to bring humanity together. I would assume human race would even pay for this convention to happen. We would pay for the building, to bring all religious leaders into the building. We would pay for the food, translators, writers, and even entertainers to facilitate the process. It would require no bloodshed what so ever. Just thousands, even millions of religious scholars working together on unified religion. Even if it took them a decade to come up with one religion; it would be the biggest gift religious leaders could have given to humanity. It would be the biggest charitable and humane achievement in thousands of years. It would create peace and love in the world that has not seen this in the longest while.

Why this religious unification hasn't happen yet? Is it too profitable to keep humanity divided? Are we that stubborn and set in our views, that we cannot find a common voice to save the human race? Surely, if all the religious leaders decided to go for it, no government and no group in the world can stop it. If your flock is like your children, how can you let them be slaughtered by thousands in a religious dispute? Isn't it the greatest parental love to settle your differences in the name of preserving sanity of your children? They certainly teach it to parents who are divorcing and pushing their different ideology of confused kids. Why not at least try to make one single religion? And I don't mean one religion taking over everything. This is way too much blood shed to have peace and love. Religious leaders should try to come together and be one. Even if they fail to do so, it is worth a shot.

While you are contemplating the idea of **ONE EARTH=ONE GOD=ONE RELIGION**, let's talk about something that might seem completely unrelated. Let's talk about Santa Clause. As a child I loved Santa Clause and there is hardly any imaginary character that gave me as much joy as he did. I looked forward to everything related to Christmas, and that is a lot considering I was not raised Christian. Christmas trees, decorations, colorful lights, and anticipation of great presents and great food, all where amazing to me. So why when I became an adult Santa Clause lost all the joy for me? I still love Christmas Trees and presents, but I am totally against telling kids to believe in Santa Clause. I want kids to know that presents come from their parents. I want them to be good for parent's sake, not for Santa's sake.

People who want their kids to believe in Santa Clause say that he is good for kids. He makes them behave better in fear of getting coal instead of their awesome presents. He is always watching for them to be good, it is a 24/7 job. He supposed to introduce some magic and wonder in kid's lives. We assume he spends most of his time in North Pole, but he is everywhere watching us. He is like a demigod, who scares kids into better behavior and buys their love with gifts and candy. What's the harm of having him then?

Well, imagine Billy whose parents pull a very modest or a low income jointly. Sure he doesn't have much. He has his older brother's hand-me-down clothes; he has a bicycle with a name no one can recognize. His school supplies are cheap, but they are all there. He doesn't have a fancy game console, but he has laptop with a name no one can recognize. He is healthy, he has all his immunizations in order, and he has not missed a day in school. He is polite and clean. He is one of the best students in his class. So his parents are doing well with him. More so, he was a great boy this whole year and Santa should bring him something great for sure. All he wants is a new cell phone like the rest of his friends. He writes the letter to Santa and waits. Christmas comes and he gets his new winter coat and boots, scarf and a warm hat. He got all the things he needs to keep him warm in winter and all the things his parents can afford. Yet, he feels like Santa hates him. His friend from a rich family got a new computer, even though he wasn't good last year at all. Next year it will seem pointless to try to be better, when he thinks Santa hates him and ignores him completely. Why someone as nice as Santa, would treat Billy so terribly wrong? The only conclusion that Billy will come to is that there is something wrong with Billy. It is shameful to give child such a mental problem over an imaginary friend. On the other hand if he knew that his parents got him the present it would be so much better. He would possibly appreciate their effort. He would possibly learn the value of money, knowing that his parents got what they could afford. He would definitely not have a mental disorder from his presents. He might even learn that a fancy winter coat bought on a tight budget is what we call parental love.

And of course magic in childhood is a major selling point for both Santa Clause and fairy tales. Why do we need it, really? People always say, "Let kids have some magic in their childhood, before they become adults and have to deal with the real world." This is how we start our lives. First, we are taught to believe in magic. Then our parents tell us that every dream we have will come true. They take us to the highest mountain peak they can find, and we stand there with the wind in our face. We believe that we can conquer any mountain and reach for even higher peaks on the distant horizon. Then there is a voice behind us that says, "Welcome to the real world!" We feel a hand on our back as we get pushed, violently, to the void below. It is a short life, but a very long drop into the abyss of reality. Same damn parents who told us that magic exists now tell us it doesn't. Same damn parents, who told us we can fly, tell us that we must come down. They tell us we must accept the world, as it is, a free-for-all fight for a bigger pile of money. We must accept the death of most of our dreams. They tell us we must prepare for a bleak future, and be incredibly surprised when this future turns out well. This is another irresponsible mind-fuck our parents impose on us. First they build us up and then they take us down. Majority of the parents are too weak, indifferent, or scared to teach us about the real world before we start living as adults. They just shut up and throw us into the world and let the world break us piece by piece. So, I ask you again why do we need magic or imaginary friends who will let us down for sure? Why can't we start living in the real world right away? Why every single adult has to come to grips with reality by falling into life like an endless abyss of disappointments? And more importantly, why adults feel the need to have an imaginary friend their whole life? Why do they feel the need to have this imaginary friend with magical powers that no human can possess? Why do we need a demigod like Santa Clause and then later in life God?

One reason could be laziness. It could be our underlining passivity and fear of making our own choices. I heard many people, especially in western religion, use this phrase: "God has a plan for me!" It is comforting to know that my creator, God, has a plan for me. Often though, when people say that God has a plan for me, they don't have their own plan for themselves. It seems like a nice excuse to live your whole life without a plan for yourself. No matter what you do everything should go according to God's plan, making your own plans not matter. Almost making any plans doesn't matter. This makes us into kids living predestined lives, with no control of our own. We spend the childhood, living for Santa's approval. And adulthood we spend living for God's approval. Either way, we don't live like masters of our own destiny. We have a very dangerous relationship with God, which even God wouldn't approve. And there are two parts to this unhealthy relationship.

One part is our insistence that human nature is evil in its core or primitive. This is mainly rooted in western religion, where our evil thoughts and deeds got us thrown out of Heaven. Heaven was the paradise and Earth is the punishment. So from the beginning, we are evil people living in the evil world. That is an awful place to start. We start as guilty and live our whole live trying to prove to God our innocence to be accepted back into Heaven. We are always presumed to be bad and terrible sinners. Some members of our society are even marginalized and made into outcasts, for simply being born who they are.

Imagine if you are a gay man or a woman. You have this urge for sexual intercourse with people of the same gender. You don't know why you feel this way; supposedly your creator gave you that urge. So God gave you desire and decided to call you evil for having this desire. He made you who you are and than made you and outcast, a person to leave behind or even kill. Imagine we have as a society where we have a group of people that God wants us to hate, even though He created them. I am not even talking about being constantly prosecuted for practicing a religion that is different from another group. It might seem, that everything we love and desire is considered a sin under religious law. Think about it, every natural urge we have is labeled primitive, evil or both. Our world seems like a heap of contradictions and hypocrisy. So much so, that I almost named this book "Mind-fuck" or "Taking crazy pills".

I REFUSE TO LIVE LIKE THIS. I REFUSE TO BE BRANDED AS EVIL FOR MY NATURAL THOUGHTS AND FEELINGS. I REFUSE THINKING ABOUT EARTH AS A PUNISHMENT. I REFUSE HAVING A LIFE IN WHICH THE BEST THINGS WILL HAPPEN TO ME ONLY WHEN I DIE AND GO TO HEAVEN. EARTH IS MY HOME AND MY HEAVEN. IT GIVES ME OXYGEN, FOOD, AND SHELTER. IT GIVES ME A PLACE TO LOVE, DREAM, AND FEEL. EARTH IS HOME AND UNIQUE. AND WE ARE THE MOST SUCCESSFUL PRODUCT OF PLANET EARTH; WE SHOULD LET OUR VANITY GO JUST THAT FAR.

Vanity. Here is an affliction, which humanity can never kick or put under control. We truly love ourselves and think that we are these unique beings molded to look like God himself or in his image. You can even say that we are much more in love with an idea of being like God than God himself. It is dangerous God Complex that we promote as a race. God suppose to be perfect. We are made in his image and are perfect by default. Sure we get naughty sometimes, but we still believe in being perfect and special. We believe that we are more significant than anything else that lives on or walks on the surface of Earth. Where can you go from here? This kind of ideology leaves no room for improvement. Why try to improve or grow as a race, if we are like perfect God? We feel so superior that our minds play tricks on us. According to the western religion, we were born in Heaven and thrown to Earth as punishment for not listening to God. This makes us almost an alien race living on planet Earth. This makes us aggressive tenants, renting and abusing our rental space. Makes us disconnected from Earth and make us feel superior to everything on Earth. I think it is much healthier to humble yourself to understanding that we are just a very successful animal species born on a planet Earth. There is plenty of magic to our existence even without God.

The fact that Earth is the only planet in our system that is habitable is magic. Us evolving from gatherers and hunters into a technologically advanced species is magic. Earth flying in space, undestroyed by numerous asteroids, is magic. Sun is magic, life giving, and not asking for anything in return.

We really don't need a classical Codependent Relationship with God. We don't need religious groups enabling this relationship. We don't need to rely on God for approval and our sense of identity and self-worth.

WE KNOW OUR SELF-WORTH. WE KNOW THAT WE CAN CREATE THE MAGIC OF OUR OWN. WE ARE THE PEOPLE WHO CREATED PLUMBING, ELECTRICITY, SHIPS TO SAIL THE OCEANS, CARS, AIRPLANES, AND SPACESHIPS. WE ARE THE PEOPLE WHO CREATED VACCINES AND ORGAN TRANSPLANTS. WE ARE THE PEOPLE WHO LEARNED TO FARM AND CREATE AMAZING FOOD. WE ARE THE PEOPLE WHO BUILT PYRAMIDS, SKYSCRAPERS, AND FANTASTIC BRIDGES, CITIES THAT LIT UP WITH MILLIONS OF LIGHTS IN THE NIGHT. WE BUILT A SOCIETY THAT CONTAINS BILLIONS OF MEMBERS AND WE ARE ON A VERGE OF LEARNING TO LIVE IN PEACE AND HARMONY WITH ONE ANOTHER.

Our lives don't need to revolve around God, who is constantly disappointed with us. No matter what we do, we will never be good enough for Him. I refuse to live as a constant disappointment to my imaginary father figure. We are good enough as people and we are better. We don't need to feel trapped in our relationship with God and try to conform to his rules and wishes. If God does exist, He cannot be a petty and jealous being. Someone so powerful, a creator, cannot draw pleasure in having obedient slaves for his children. He cannot enjoy mindless and passive obedience and faith. Why give us a brain and tell us not to think? Why give us hearts and tell us not to feel? And why give us eyes, just to tell us to turn a blind eye?

I refuse to live in Codependent Relationship with God, where I have to smile and accept everything that is happening no matter how awful. I don't want to accept good people dying or being bullied and abused as part of a master plan. I don't want to sing praises to God, even if I feel that he is ruining my life instead of making it better. ***WE SHOULDN'T LIVE OUR LIVES TO PLEASE GOD. WE SHOULD LIVE OUR LIVES TO PLEASE EACH OTHER.*** In a way, we are putting too much pressure and responsibility on God. If he exists, he can't possibly care about each and single life. I honestly believe in this saying: "God helps those, who help themselves." Sitting on your ass and waiting for a miracle never works. ***LOVE, HARD WORK, DEDICATION, AND BELIEVING IN OURSELVES IS THE ONLY WAY FOR US TO CREATE OUR OWN MIRACLES.***

With all the things I said above, I have to admit that once I was God. When I was in high school I bought my first and last aquarium. It was glorious rectangular masterpiece. I laid little stones of different color on the bottom. I put in a castle with numerous caves; a broken pirate ship with logs and holes to swim through. Hooked up the air. Set up a shining light to give warms. Bought my first bag of fish food and my first batch of citizens. They were really fun to play with. I named every single fish I got and I stayed long enough by the tank to learn something about his or her tiny personalities. I knew which fish liked to swim all the time and which fish liked to stay in the cave dreaming. I knew which fish liked to pick fights and which fish liked to eat too much. I would tap on the glass and they would move their lips, as if in silent prayer. They would swim around, which would look like a beautiful dance. When I fed them they would line up and wiggle their happy tails. I would talk to them and reward them with extra food when they listened. I would come from school and watch them for while and then I would go to bed. In the beginning it was fun.

Then I realized how much work it was and it wasn't as much fun as it was before. I would forget to change the water or feed my little friends. When the first one died and was floating belly up, I was very sad for few hours. It wasn't so bad with 2 or 3rd one. When I got a new batch, I didn't even name them. There was no point in naming them. They were dying too fast. I did get a little net, and I would catch the little, nameless, dead fish and send it on its toilet bowl adventure. After a while, I got so busy with school and dating I had no time for my fish friends. So when the last one died, I didn't get a new batch and threw away the whole aquarium. The spot on the table was just right for my new computer, anyway. I guess I was a bad God or just regular one. It could also be my age of no reason and teenage hormones that prevented me from being a good God.

Men and women grow up at different maturity rate. Women are expected to be caregivers and makers of the nest we call home. They are expected to care for children and cook food. Even female toys revolve around dolls, fake cups and dishes, and fake ovens. Maybe this is the main reason women tend to mature faster then men. For men the maturity curve is long. I would say male brain reaches its maturity after thirty years of age. It happened to me too. I was at my grandfather's funeral looking at my family in tears. Cursing myself for never being able to cry, even if my heart was breaking into pieces. Two and a half generations above the ground and half of the oldest generation below. I looked at them thinking what is value of all of our lives? One moment we are crying over a family member, then few years or few decades later and our family is crying over us. Hundreds of stones around me, with names of people who lived and died unnoticed by most. Their lives were important only to a very small group who knew them well. Generations of invisible people and whose graves will even disappear with time. It goes by fast, I thought. Did they live their dream before they died? Did they dare to live their dreams? And if it goes by so fast, is there a point to live in misery and fear? Shouldn't we all strive to live in a better world? If it goes by so fast, why we waist time on hate, when all we want is love? Standing there I had no answers, but I knew I had to search for them. It happened so fast and so strong, that the weight of the information almost crushed me. I assume everyone gets their own moment and their own experience that sets things in motion. Something inside clicks and the picture becomes clear. The world seems to make less sense, but it is clearly visible to our minds. Understanding rolls in and paints your life with bright visible colors. You see all your mistakes you made in the past. You might even see some you would make in your future. You see your life path like a yellow brick road winding through life obstacles. People around you start to fall in two distinct groups, those who make your life better and those who make your life worse. There is something very philosophical about this clarity. It is so clear that it is almost scary. It produces this sucking fear that screams for action, for purpose, for a meaning in our lives. Women like to call this a mid-life crisis, and blame men for trying to relive their youth. This is a wrong read. Sure some men will find meaning in sex, some will find it in expensive toys like cars and boats. Some will even try to push their body beyond its age limits. Ultimately it is a philosophical moment for most men. It is a moment for most men to choose a direction and decide what meaning their life has on this Earth. It is no surprise, that this moment of clarity is responsible for many great men throughout history. It is very curious that all the religious figures either began their journey or did their best work between the ages of 30 and 40. This is very true of Buddha, Jesus, Muhammad, Moses, Horus. They were mature men who wanted their life to matter. They wanted to follow a meaningful and selfless path, while inspiring others to do the same. Could it be, that they saw the world they lived in and wanted to make it better? Could it be, that they had to make up God so people would listen and follow their teachings? And finally, is it possible that the only peaceful way to make people listen was inventing an all-powerful imaginary friend?

Plan de Vida (Life Plan)

The most irresponsible and heartless thing we do is letting our kids inherit the world that we know will make them miserable. For thousands of years, generation after generation we seem to be not able to break the wheel of misery. We tell our kids we love them, and for the most part we mean it. Still, no generation is willing to sacrifice themselves to change the pattern of passing along to kids their own prejudices, antiquated believes, fears, bigotry, and hopelessness. The biggest problem with our society is that our biggest fools are our greatest prophets. And our greatest prophets are our biggest fools. We don't have enough honest, unbiased voices out there to guide us to a better future. We tell ourselves that we are powerless against those in power. We tell ourselves that wealthy interests, who are not interested in change, drown brave voices. We stay passive out of fear and many unsuccessful examples from the past. We even have a name for a perfect society. We call it utopia. We don't believe in a perfect society and by doing so kill any chance of creating one, but the only way to achieve something great is believing in it yourself. And when your beliefs are strong, you turn others around you into believers. **BELIEVING IN IMPOSSIBLE AS POSSIBLE IS WHAT MAKES US A GREAT SPECIES.** And we shouldn't be afraid to change our lives for better. We get one life on this Earth and it is awful to waist this short time on making each other miserable.

Unfortunately, being passive is no longer an option. Air travel has changed our lives forever. In a way, traveling by plane has erased all the borders and separations by land or ocean. Any disease can get on the plane and travel the world with in days and can become a global epidemic. Armies can reach any place in the world, and no place is safe and excluded in its microcosm. We live in the age of mobile war and mobile disease. With the invention of Internet, our lives became even more connected and less isolated. Any form of ideology, good or bad, can travel through the Internet in seconds. It can reach the furthest ends of the world as long as there is electricity there. At the same time, world economies got intertwined and financial matters of each country are no longer isolated. A financial crash or a bad economic decision in one country can send ripples around the world affecting other countries. Even bad political decisions made in one country can send a shock wave of problems around the globe.

So, we must think globally from now on. **YOU MUST SAY TO YOURSELF: "FIRST AND MOST IMPORTANTLY, I AM A MEMBER OF HUMAN RACE AND A CITIZEN OF EARTH." EVERYTHING ELSE MUST COME SECOND.** You must ask yourself, what is better for the human race? Which ever will benefit humanity, will also benefit you! You must ask yourself, what it means to be a citizen of Earth? Earth is a home to us all. Being a good citizen should mean never doing anything to destroy your home. It also means leaving home in good shape for generations to come. And finally, we must fall in love with the word **UNITY**. United we are unstoppable and unbeatable. Divided we will fall and perish from the face of this Earth. In order for us to survive, we must fall in love with another great word: **FOCUS**. We need to understand that our energy is not endless, and cannot be wasted on stupid causes and unnecessary discussion. We must work to figure out the most important goals and focus on them.

ONLY THROUGH UNITY AND FOCUS CAN WE BECOME AN ENLIGHTENED RACE WE ALWAYS DREAMED OF BEING!

And as my part to get the ball rolling I will conclude this book with some possible ideas and solutions we can bring to life. I read way too many philosophical books that never offered any ideas or solutions to take into the real world. As great and as insightful as they were, they were useless at the end. We need to have a plan. We need to focus on the main points of the plan and push as one towards achieving such a plan. I don't have all the answers, I am sure of it. And humbly, propose that I found some answers. I shared some through the book already and I will give you most important ones now.

Let us start with our society as a whole. Again, any society is a contract made to live a life a certain way. Like any contract it can be renegotiated and it can be altered and updated. It can even be rewritten anew and be totally different from a previous one we made. Life is fluid and is always changing and moving forward. We have to move forward with life and constantly update the contract. Things that once were "normal" like slavery are now totally against the law, and I hope it stays that way. Humanity always tries to practice a version of slavery, like inhumane factory work or inescapable financial traps. Being gay was once was normal, then it became sinfully wrong, and now it is normal again. Hopefully, we never ever again prosecute consenting adults for the kind of sex they prefer. Killing people once was normal, then it was a sin, and now it is normal again, as long as it is done for higher profits. Either normal or abnormal, killing people was always in style. Unfortunately, killing is the only way we truly know how to settle any large dispute. And why not kill each other for no reason? We are so divided as a society that all we produce are conflicts and disputes.

According to www.worldometers.info there are ***195 countries in the world in 2017***. Also according to Encyclopedia Britannica in 1911, there were 1000 languages spoken in the world. And according to Ethnologue catalog ***in 2009 there are 6,909 distinct languages in the world***. Even if there are projections that about half of these languages will go in the next century, it is still too many. Anything above 1 language seems like too much. Nothing facilitates communication better than having the same language. This is another great project we have not undertaken yet: ***"ONE HUMANITY = ONE LANGUAGE"***. Here is a chance for the linguists to feel supremely important and benefit humanity immensely in the process. All their knowledge can be gathered in one giant facility and finally put to work to unify humanity. They could work day and night with every language out there, to create a melting pot of words and writing styles. And after few years of tedious labor, we will have a new language. We will call it Terrian. It will be the new universal language taught in school and each youngster would need to know Terrian well. It might take 2 or 3 generations, but Terrian will become the only language. Books will be written in it and everyone will talk and sing exclusively in Terrian. Government documents and daily news all will be produced in Terrian. We will no longer have a language barrier to keep us separated. And we will be one step closer to unifying humanity, hopefully without bloodshed.

When it comes to "United Nations", it was a great idea in the right direction. Unfortunately, people see United Nations like a dog without teeth. We are sort of afraid of it, but wonder what it can really do to stop us. With 195 countries out there and them having their 195 distinct interests, United Nations seems to be failing to bring them together. **MAYBE THE FAILURE IS IN THE NAME "UNITED NATIONS" ITSELF. PERSONALLY I LIKE UNITED EARTH BETTER.** United Nations as a name implies numerous national (separate) interests brought to one table. It feels like the name itself creates borders and separations, which were a problem in the first place. United Earth would be a borderless organization in charge of laws that govern our society and it would set the standards of living for the whole Earth population. Each nation would be required to dissolve most of its army and the remainder would be absorbed into the army protecting Earth. The new army would be called **TERRAGUARDS** and they would answer to United Earth only. Their job would be just to train and prepare for any extraterrestrial threats and act as Earth police. With borders between nations erased, it would be only natural to introduce single currency. This would make financial matters seamless and unified and ultimately easier. Instead of pictures of kings and presidents on the new bank notes, we will put pictures of famous scientists and citizens, who changed world history for the better. Imagine Nikola Tesla, Albert Einstein, Alexander Fleming, Marie Curie, Galileo Galilei, Coco Chanel, Johannes Gutenberg, Amelia Mary Earhart, and Wright Brothers on our money. Every bank note will celebrate their amazing achievements and discoveries. Every bank note will describe on the back the way these people changed humanity forever and for better. And if some names I mentioned seem unfamiliar, search them out on the Internet. I promise you, behind each name there is an amazing life and amazing work, worth emulating.

A leader of each nation will have to give up his standing for a seat on United Earth governing floor. They forever more will become heroes to their people, they will have monuments, buildings and schools named after them, and they will have museums dedicated to them. Each leader will spend the rest of his life well respected and wealthy, humanity will make sure of that. The sacrifice of power by each leader will be the greatest deed a leader in history ever accomplished. We will leave these leaders as giants in our history. And every child will learn in school about the Brave 200 (195 at current standing) that sacrificed their role for a better tomorrow. Each region, specifically, will study their own leader's life in detail. So the leaders will not go into obscurity, and they will work on shaping humanity while living by representing their region in United Earth. If set up correctly, the economic advantages of joining United Earth would outweigh any petty local interests. Each former nation will become a region or a state, with the promise that EVERY region will have EQUAL opportunities and standards of living. United Earth will also create millions of jobs building infrastructure and updating technology around the globe.

Think of what we got so far. It is a careful step-by-step process, which could yield a united humanity. We start by pushing for a single language, Terrian. Once we get that, we can start a push for the single governing body United Earth. Then we can make the next step and form a single army, Terraguards. And at the same time we would work on a single currency, which we would call **TERRABUCKS**. Step by step we would have unified Earth population making all our interests united. We would set standards of living that would have to be equal and decent everywhere. The magic word here is **INCLUSION**. We all want to have certain comforts of life that right now are not universal at all. Things like plumbing, healthy food, clean water, comfortable housing, affordable health care, and being able to work and live in peace are far from being universal. Opportunities to learn and grow financially are not universal. In the current state of things, we have many people excluded from some or all needed comforts of live. Exclusion breeds envy and hate. Exclusion makes people feel substandard and forgotten. You cannot have a strong, united humanity where only some people enjoy the gifts of life.

By the way, we already solved the problem of terrorism in the world; we just forgot that we did. We insist on using blind force and we are just wasting time with no serious results. Force only causes fear, which is temporary and produces extreme hate and rebellions. Force and fear marginalizes people, while love is a very inclusive feeling. Actually, a single United States company solved the problem with a fizzy, sugary drink. This company figured out the power of the inclusion very early. As soon as I learned the word Coca-colonization in college, it became one of my absolute favorite words. The word refers to how Coca-Cola© company used its beverage to colonize the world with American way of life. Coca-cola© company spread though Europe after World War II putting its product in the hands of European youth. With the beverage, people got to know and like American culture. Drinking Cola made people feel like they are included in the way of living they liked and wanted to emulate. A fizzy caffeine and sugar beverage built a connection between cultures and made people like American way of living and made them our friends. After all, why would you want to blow up the country, which makes your favorite beverage? Why would you want to blow up a country, which has a way of living you admire? All this was

achieved without a single bullet or a bomb, just by the power of
inclusion. That is why it is so important to unify the human race.
We want everyone to be happy, while living on Earth.

This brings me to the meaning of life. The biggest angst for
the human race lies in a single question: Why are we here? We
always feel like we are meant for something more than what we
are right now. We are always looking for some complex solution.
We imagine ourselves as lost children of God or lost alien race
that was left on Earth. And all these solutions are so disconnected
from our real lives, that they only bring marginal comfort. It still
leaves us with the Why? It still leaves us without a purpose we
can follow? I believe the answer is simple, just not that easy to
achieve:

**THE MEANING OF LIFE IS TO LEARN TO
LIVE IN PEACE AND HARMONY WITH ONE
ANOTHER, AND FOR HUMANITY TO UNITE
AS ONE. AND AS UNITED HUMAN RACE,
WE MUST FURTHER OUR KNOWLEDGE
AND TECHNOLOGY, SPREADING
THROUGH UNIVERSE AND SHARING OUR
ACHIEVEMENTS.**

Of course, achieving this goal is not easy. Once we are
unified, we are still in danger of loosing it. We need a deeper plan
and understanding of what we must do. We must have a moral
code or a way of living that will guide all our decisions in the right
direction.

The trick with ethics and morality is that it seems natural or
inherent, but it always needs to be enforced by law. Certain things
seem right, but they are not so in real life. For example, killing
and raping is extremely wrong, without a shadow of a doubt.
They are so wrong that no one needs to tell you they are so, yet
we still have to make laws to punish this kind of terrible behavior.

It also feels right that scientists, teachers, and doctors should be the highest paid professions. It seems right that these people, which shape our world, will be the stars of humanity. It seems right, but we know it is not so. Most of the people we put value on are people with good looks, regardless of their contribution to the world. Also when you talk about ethics of the society, you have to talk about freedom. The idea of absolute freedom is often contradictory to moral or ethical code, because it is a fairy tail idea.

Society in which there is absolute freedom is an impossible dream. It is anarchy and madness. In an absolutely free society I can come up to anyone on the street and shoot him or her in the face with no consequences for me. People, in general, can shit into the water supply and not show up for work. People can steal from each other, beat and rape one another at will. People can burn forests and kill off species of animals all without consequences. You cannot have anarchy and a functioning society at the same time. Nothing will get done and our lives will be even crazier then they are now.

Society needs rules. Of course, these rules will impinge on your "absolute freedom", but in return you get a better life. The trick is what rules we agree on? And what moral or ethical code we use to guide us in shaping our new brave world? I don't see a better place to start than to talk about Epigenetics.

Epigenetics is the study of potentially heritable changes in gene expression. These changes, or traits or phenotypes, do not involve changes in the underlying DNA. Still these changes have damaging effects and can result in diseases like cancer. Furthermore, the environment we live in can affect these changes. This is what concerns me the most. Our environment, the way we are raised and the state of the world around us, can affect our genes. It doesn't change the DNA, but it does activate or silence certain genes. And the Epigenetic changes can be transmitted to further generations as a terrible or great heritage. Something like food and traumatic experience have a potential of changing our genes, and thus genes of our children to come. To me it means that the environment we live in can make us better or worse. I new our environment can have the ability to change our behavior, but changes on the gene level are even scarier.

We all know what happens to human morality when faced with fear and hunger. Feeling afraid and hungry switches on the survival mode and completely overrides any moral code we have. This has been used widely in politics to steer people to make decisions against their better judgment. Fear and hunger are so strong that it has been a main reason why people are settling for lives way below normal standards or their expectations. This is the very reason why FOOD, SHELTER and SAFETY are at the base of my *EVOLUTION OF HUMAN NEEDS PYRAMID*.

WITHOUT PEACEFUL AND WELL-FED ENVIRONMENT, THERE IS NO CHANCE OF PRODUCING A HIGHLY SOPHISTICATED, MORALLY STABLE SOCIETY. WHEN YOU APPLY THIS TOGETHER WITH EPIGENETICS, THERE IS A STRONG POSSIBILITY THAT LIVING IN A HOSTILE ENVIRONMENT CAN PRODUCE BROKEN OR DISEASED PEOPLE. WE ARE ALL JUST AS MUCH A PRODUCT OF OUR PARENTS DNA, AS WE ARE PRODUCT OF THE ENVIRONMENT IN WHICH WE WERE RAISED.

What if the polluted and chemically induced food we eat changed us on a gene level? Does it have an ability to make us more prone to cancer? What if our scary world changed us on a gene level? What if living in constant fear of death and famine, made us incapable of love or made us afraid of love? And if it is true, are we capable of being better people? I wrote this book, because I believe we still have a chance to build a better society. I wrote this book thinking that if we build a better society, it will in turn create a better human race. We just have to be fearless in our decisions and our determination to leave the old world behind.

And so, we must speak about religion again. And since religion branded itself as keepers of our ethics and moral code, it is very important in our discussion of unifying human race. As it stands now, religion is a serious threat to our unification as human race. As optimistic as I am, I still feel that it would be almost impossible for all religions to settle their differences and come together as one. Imagine my surprise that a man living in 19th century also thought this way. He even wrote a book, which will celebrate its 200th birthday in year 2020. I am talking about *Thomas Jefferson* and his book *The Life and Morals of Jesus of Nazareth*. Thomas Jefferson was very devoted to teachings of Jesus Christ, but he believed that Jesus morality could be useful without mentioning all the miraculous events and cut them out of his book. He believed that many religious followers corrupted the Christ morality with their schismatizing (producing division or separation from church) believes and teachings. Thomas Jefferson also believed in Deism. And Deism is a believe system that accepts an existence of a creator. It rejects the idea that the creator is some kind of supernatural deity who talks to people from time to time. It also rejects the idea that the creator constantly interferes in human life. Deism believes in a creator that lets the universe run itself, basically leaving our future in our hands. All in all, Thomas Jefferson was on the right track of trying to unify humanity. He was also on the right track on believing that we build our own future and our destiny. 200 years later we are still far away from both ideas.

Now, what if we have to abandon religion to save the human race? What source will we use to draw our morals? What will be our ethical guide? Can we even create one, based on what we know already? Well, I decided to undertake the risky business of putting it on paper. It probably is not complete, but it should do as a starting point for minds better than mine to expand on. I went with ideas that simply make sense to me. And I went with ideas that seem to make sense from perspective of loving human race. I have divided them into three groups: **ABSOLUTELY WRONG, TERRIAN BIRTH RIGHTS, AND TERRIAN ADULT RIGHTS AND RESPONSIBILITIES.**

ABSOLUTELY WRONG

Humanity in general has a great proclivity for violence. We only don't like violence when it happens to us. We only hate accidents that happen to us. When violence and accidents happens to other people it's either news or videos we watch. I sincerely hope that we will outlive the violent side, by replacing it with an advanced intellect. It might take few generations of intellectual growth to get this point. For now, we have to repeat this mantra to ourselves over and over again: "People don't kill people, unless it is in self-defense and your own life is threatened!"

For the society to come, here are the three basic wrongs:

You are not to bring harm to yourself or to any other human being.

This article includes in itself not killing other people, unless it is in self-defense and your life is threatened. It also includes not committing suicide as a way of getting out of emotional problems. Where assisted suicide in terminally ill patients is a mercy and relief of terrible pain. Any other reason to commit suicide is a weak move. There is nothing brave or noble in avoiding facing your problems and fighting for your own life. This article also includes stealing from others. Stealing has no place and no need in an enlightened society. No citizen should suffer the pain of another citizen living of him or her and not contributing to the society.

You are not to bring harm to the environment.

This article includes in itself not polluting air, soil, or water. It includes a ban on manufacturing environmentally harmful products. It includes severe punishment for killing animals and destroying forests for sport. We are not masters of nature; we are a part of nature and should act as such. And we must treat our unique planet with respect.

It is absolutely wrong for a law to delegate respect.

Whether it is religious or government law, it should not delegate respect. Respect must be earned based on actions and not political position or advanced age. No politician or leader must have our respect, just because he or she is in charge. This is how we make kings and queens out of ordinary people. Elderly shouldn't be respected simply because they are old. You can respect their age by giving up your seat in a crowded transportation. You can respect their age by providing them with pension and much needed medical care. Respecting a person individually shouldn't be automatic with age. A young asshole will be and elderly asshole, the only thing that will change is age. Some people gain wisdom with age. Some people stay clueless forever. We advance by rebelling against old believes and ideas or testing them for validity. We should not mix civil behavior with forced respect and mindless obedience.

TERRIAN BIRTH RIGHTS

Every child born on Earth is automatically an Earth citizen with all citizen rights.

Every citizen from birth is master of his or her body.

And nobody has the right to violate the body of child or an adult for that matter. And nobody has the right to tell an adult what to do with his or her body. (No body of government has a right to outlaw anything like abortions or assisted suicides for terminally ill patients. Even regulating pregnancy in emergency seems like a very wrong power to put in someone's hands. One of the forbidden children might end up the most important citizen we need and never will have. If you set up the society correctly, we shouldn't need to worry about extra citizens. If we will decide to settle on other planets, we will need these citizens to settle those planets.)

Every Earth citizen is entitled to free Medical Care for life.
Government will retain a percent of individual's yearly salary to raise funds for the free service provided to the citizen.

Every Earth citizen is entitled to free access to food, water, and housing.

Government will retain a percent of individual's yearly salary to raise funds for the free service provided to the citizen.

Every Earth citizen is entitled to free education and free access to the knowledge base being stored in libraries.

Free education will include school and college and advanced degrees. Since education is a key to a liberated and enlightened human race, it will finally receive funding and attention it deserves. Libraries will be updated and computerized to make any information well protected and easily referenced by citizens. Government will retain a percent of individual's yearly salary to raise funds for the free service provided to the citizen.

Every Earth citizen is entitled to paid retirement after 35 to 40 years of working and keeping society going.

The paid retirement will include money and medical care required by the citizen. Every citizen must feel that his or her lifetime contribution to the society has value and is appreciated. Government will retain a percent of individual's yearly salary, during the years of service, to raise funds for the free service provided to the citizen.

TERRIAN ADULT RIGHTS AND RESPONSIBILITIES

Every Terrian citizen must abide by laws, which delegate cooperation, sharing of the resources, and preserve health and safety of the human race. Citizens should be encouraged to contribute to the society by providing physical or intellectual work. Individual contribution must be a matter of pride, civic duty, and a way to give each individual life a purpose.

Every provider of food should be well compensated and strictly regulated to make sure a healthy chemical-free, hormone-free food supply.

Also government will work on providing a very detailed education about proper food consumption and well balanced diet.

Every Terrian citizen must have access to free sports centers and be encouraged to use them as much as possible.

Healthy bodies lead to healthy minds and physically strong population. Healthy citizens need less medical care. We can break the wheel of making people sick with bad food and no exercise and trying to fix them later with medications.

Every Terrian must have freedom of speech.

This is something we should never give up. Evil only wins if it stays in the shadows and good people do nothing. Words will always inspire people. And being exposed to multitude of opinions is the only way to sort out truth from a beautiful lie.

Sexual Freedom must never be removed from law.

There will always be ideologies and groups trying to control sex or label kinds of sex as normal or abnormal. Know that what they are trying to do is by controlling your sexual expression; they are trying to control your body and ultimately control you. All you need to know is that CONSENSUAL SEX between two ADULTS needs no regulation. Rape and any other way of forcing your sexual desire on someone who does not want it can and must be outlawed. Outlawing any consensual sex is flat out wrong. There are many sexual acts that I personally will find not enjoyable or even disgusting. Yet, there is no need to outlaw them just retain my right to not participate in them personally.

This is all I can come up with, so far, as a starter guide to the future us. It seems to me that if you start with love and understanding, you can easily focus on the rules that society needs. If you add to that putting value on each life, rules are really writing themselves on the page. For too long we have been living by rules that only benefit a small percent of society. Building a great future is very hard. We must learn not to settle for less and always strive to be the race that puts human lives first.

One way to put human lives first is to fight for Sexual Freedom or fixing the third pillar of the **EVOLUTION OF HUMAN NEEDS PYRAMID**. What can we do?

We can utilize our power of masses. And we do have power, regardless of how it feels right now. How about from now on and until it is achieved, every politician MUST make sexual freedom as his or hers main issue. How about him or her signing a binding contract, since we love contracts so much. If the politician doesn't push for sexual freedom, under the contract, he or she must resign from office. How about a social media initiated world strike in the name of sexual freedom. A total stand still for the world economy, costing billions of dollars, until we people get what we want. Maybe loosing money will force the discussion in our favor and get things done. After all, we will not be asking anybody to give up power. All we will be asking is not to be persecuted for consensual sex. All we will be asking is not to be prosecuted for controlling our own body. It seems like an easy bone to throw to the populace, without changing everything too drastically. They already giving us drugs and alcohol to forget our problems, now we will be able to fuck our problems away.

Or how about this, United Nation has to prove to us that it is very effective organization and will create a worldwide push for Terrian Language. Let's setup an island away from all politics and have linguist work there to create a new language. Where United Nation will come in, is a promise that the project will be funded by all nations. It will also make sure that the language will be integrated into the school programs everywhere as a second language. This project requires no wars, just funding and negotiation.

Once Sexual Freedom is achieved and Terrian language is created, we might have a world more receptive to other more advance changes. At the very least, we can say that we are the generation that has put a crack in a wheel. It is too hard to break it right away, but a crack in a wheel is a great start.

One last discussion before I leave you alone with your thoughts. I want to discuss SCIENCE, which is our main tool in pushing society forward. At first glance, it seems that scientific expression needs no regulation and no bounds. Then you think of wars, atomic bombs, poisonous gases, bacterial warfare and you start to think of science as a two-edged sword. This sword can either protect humanity or destroy it; the key lies in the use. With that mind, I thought it would be wonderful to talk about focus in the world of science.

As much as I hate creating regulating bodies, which can be corrupted with time. Science needs some control. Just creating something because you can, without thinking of consequences or usefulness, is wrong and dangerous. I have created this acronym **SBH (SCIENCE BENEFITING HUMANITY)**. SBH can be a panel of very gifted, brilliant scientists, like a large peer review group. Their function would be to regulate, focus, and celebrate human scientific expression. Every project will need to prove that it will benefit human race and it is worth working on. There is no need to spend money and energy researching the obvious or trying to discover something that will rain destruction on us. SBH would receive a request to work on a project and members of the panel would vote on it going forward or not. Another possible function would be suggesting possible areas of discovery and projects to work on. Also SBH would release a publication celebrating yearly discoveries and people behind them. Another great function would be a holiday once a year celebrating discoveries that saved humanity or made humanity great, science discoveries that benefited the human race. This would be a great way to make scientist into rock stars of our society, something every kid would dream to be. Also I would hope that SBH would create a focus for creations that only benefit us and make us stronger and better.

With SBH in mind, let's talk about AI. In all honesty, do we really need artificial intelligence? Are we putting enough work on expanding our own intelligence? Human brain is roughly 2-3 % of the body weight, yet it uses up to 20% of body energy. It is the organ that is responsible for the greatness of our race. Yet it seems like growing brains is a slow process for human race. 1.8 million years ago it was about 600 ml, 500,000 years ago it was 1,000 ml, and now it is roughly 1,200 to 1,400 ml. *IT WOULD BE GREAT FOR SCIENCE TO WORK ON EXPANDING THE SIZE OF THE HUMAN BRAIN AND POSSIBLY WORK ON MAXIMIZING OUR OWN INTELLIGENCE.* To me it seems like a better area of focus. With each leap in intelligence we should become a better, more enlightened humanity.

Artificial Intelligence seems like an expression of human laziness. First, we have created computers and they have we been very beneficial for us, yet it seems like we are getting tired of running them. We want them to run themselves. We want them to learn, adopt, and make their own conclusions. We want them to analyze the data and predict future. Did we ask ourselves why would and autonomous computer need us? For AI we are a substandard burden, a lesser race. With AI we are creating one of two things. We either creating our own electronic monster, which will rule human race and eventually discard it, or we are creating a race of electronic slaves. I read about the current research trying to replicate the human brain and a robot capable of composing music on its very own. Maybe in my ignorance I am missing something. It seems unnecessary to have robots composing music. Music is one of the greatest gifts that was ever given to human race and we are itching to give it away.

Again, why do we need an autonomous electronic brain learning and making its decisions about its place in our society? Right now our mental superiority keeps us at the top of the food chain. Creating something superior to us will make us either slaves or expandable. It is a dangerous route with horrible payoff at the end.

And if we are not slaves ourselves, like I said before; people always try to create a form of slavery. I get it. There are certain things people don't like to do. Things like removing garbage and human wastes is first thing that comes to mind. Farming and cooking seems like too much for us too. Really, any heavy labor or any badly smelling labor seems like too much for us. Still, it would be great to have a machine do it, but a machine a person must supervise and control. Are we really so lazy that we don't even want to supervise the labor. We should never create anything that is so much better than us, that it doesn't need us. A completely autonomous electronic slave will realize that it will be better of as a master. Creating autonomy is like creating freedom. And you can't create free slaves. Artificial Intelligence might be very useful in some fields like medicine, but it should be very well controlled and well reserved in its reach. A supercomputer will not save us, if we cannot save ourselves.

With respect to garbage and human waste. We should really put a lot of effort into making this process clean and efficient. Human waste in any form needs to be converted into energy, fertilizer, or even ash. Removing it efficiently will reduce disease and make living cleaner for the environment and us. It just seems like something so basic, and is also not getting enough focus in our scientific world. I understand that human shit and garbage don't make for fun research, but it something we produce in large amounts every day. Imagine that we can create bathrooms and kitchens capable of converting human waste into energy. And we can use this energy to run the house. With good funding and focus, we can make plumbing and landfills obsolete and antiquated relics of the past.

My final point on science has to do with space travel. This has been my most sacred dream as a human being. I always thought it would be magical to discover new planets and new people. Since, it will not be possible in my lifetime, I sincerely wish it would be possible for generations to come. And to me, space exploration has to have two main areas of focus. First, we can't reach any new planets on current fuel. We need to work tirelessly on a new, much more efficient form of fuel. It should not be few governments or few billionaires working on this. We need a whole humanity and all of our best minds working on it. Only by creating a new super fuel, we can reach our second goal. And the second goal should be searching Universe for habitable new planets to live on. With our population growing we must discover these frontiers to save humanity. It is great to try to reach for Mars and it would be more important to reach for planets outside of our solar system that can be populated due to friendly oxygen and water. Fuel is the main focus in all respects. Even running things here on Earth efficiently and cleanly is a great challenge. It seems like all it needs is just more funding and focus to create one. We seem to be close to something and yet not close enough yet. It almost seems like a race. Will the old forms of fuel kill us off or stop being available, before we create new and better ones?

Remember our purpose as human race; it is simple in its wisdom. Even Aristotle, living in ancient Greece in 300s BC, had a grasp on what is the purpose of human life. It's Eudaimonia. And Eudaimonia just means that the purpose of human life is happiness and flourishing of humanity. So let us focus all our energy and all our efforts and live to make the entire human race happy. Let's live each day to make this world a place that only maximizes the happiness and intelligence of the entire Terrian race.

Unapologetic Manifesto

Few more words to the future us...

For the generations to come, I want to leave you with a final thought. When you will sit down to write the rules that will change our world in the future, I know it will not be easy. I know you will face resistance and you, most likely, will have to fight for the new and better society. Still, when you will start putting rules together, remember that rules are like clothing. Sometimes clothes look right on a hanger and feel wrong on your body or will start to choke you with their tightness. Sometimes clothes look absolutely unappealing on a hanger and fit you like a glove, making sense with every curve of your body. Ultimately, someone will hate and someone will love each single piece of clothing. And just like you can't make clothes that appeal to everyone, you can't make rules that everyone will like. All you can do is have your love for human race as a guide. And if you write each rule with people's happiness and wellbeing in mind, you should come up with some great ones.

Unapologetic Manifesto

Write your own thoughts and ideas here. I am sure that they will be useful for the future humanity:

Made in the USA
Columbia, SC
01 August 2020

14475269R00078